Library of
Davidson College

Utopian Literature

Advisory Editor:
ARTHUR ORCUTT LEWIS, JR.
Professor of English
The Pennsylvania State University

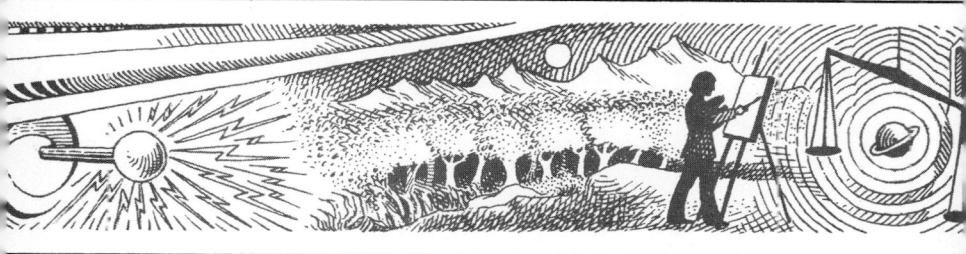

Looking Beyond

Ludwig A. Geissler

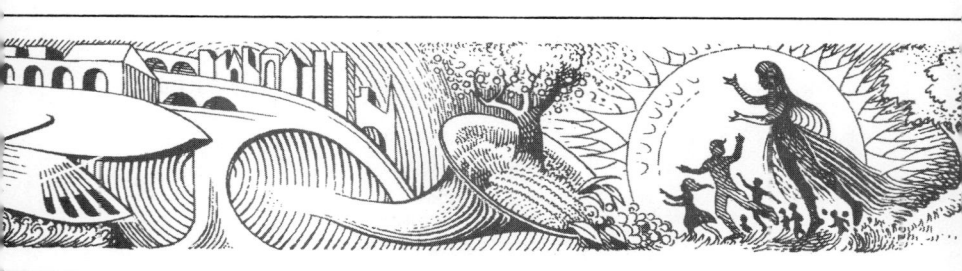

ARNO PRESS & THE NEW YORK TIMES
NEW YORK • 1971

828
G 313 l

Reprint Edition 1971 by Arno Press Inc.

Reprinted from a copy in The Pennsylvania State University Library

LC# 75-154442
ISBN 0-405-03525-X

Utopian Literature
ISBN for complete set: 0-405-03510-1

Manufactured in the United States of America

83 - 8177

LOOKING BEYOND.

LOOKING BEYOND,

A SEQUEL TO "LOOKING BACKWARD,"
BY EDWARD BELLAMY.

AND

AN ANSWER TO "LOOKING FURTHER FORWARD,"
BY RICHARD MICHAELIS.

BY

L. A. GEISSLER

London:
WILLIAM REEVES, 83 CHARING CROSS ROAD, W.C.

PRINTED BY THE NEW TEMPLE PRESS NORBURY CRESCENT, S.W.16.

PREFACE.

It is and always was one of the tactics of conservative minds tauntingly to challenge social reformers: "If you have so much to say about the evils of our present system, show us how the system you advocate would work!"

This, in his book, "Looking Backward," Mr. Bellamy very ably has done. Of course, the author of that book never made pretension of being a prophet or a dictator, decreeing laws for future generations; his idea evidently was to show in a series of pictures how, by general and scientific co-operation, an equitable system could be instituted, the thousandfold misery of human beings tainting the present system be abolished, and the welfare of all individuals of the human species be accomplished. If this was his object, he certainly was successful, and the immense circulation of "Looking Backward" shows that he struck a chord in the hearts of American and English speaking people.

Since then a book appeared, "Looking Further Forward," by R. Michaelis, in which the author, continuing the thread of the story where Mr. Bellamy left off, attempts to show that the system advocated in "Looking Backward" would lead to the utter ruin of humanity and civilisation He gives drastic descriptions of misery and dejection, corruption and humiliation, consequent on such social and political arrangements, and contrasts favourably the present system to the one advocated by Mr. Bellamy. In these attempts the author's style of argumentation is decidedly unfair. He quotes numerous sentences of Mr. Bellamy's book (giving the number of the page in footnotes), independent from their former connections, in such arrangements as to arbitrarily suit his own purposes. Notwithstanding these unfair means, his argumentation is weak and shallow, which I intend to prove.

The particulars of what the future will bring are hidden from our knowledge, but anyone who can read the signs of our time must see that the present system of *competition*, which secures my happiness by the misery of my neighbour, is doomed, and that our era is impregnate with the germ of a more equitable system, a system of *general co-operation*, a system in which the welfare of one is the welfare of all. Any observant mind can see that we are in the midst of revolution, that the former system of individual competition is more and more superseded by a system of combination, in which the financially strongest expropriate the financially weaker, and it naturally follows that the time will come, when the expropriators will be expropriated by the people. Whether this future state of society will be accomplished by independent groups with voluntary cooperation or by centralisation, the future will tell. Mr. Bellamy in his book has given a picture of the latter, and in the following treatise I shall adopt the same course for the sake of argument.

In "Looking Beyond" I mean to show the fallacies of Mr. Michaelis's arguments. I shall use the same form as Mr. Bellamy and Mr. Michaelis, treating "Looking Further Forward" as a continuation of "Looking Backward," and shall resume the thread of the narrative accordingly.

All quotations from Mr. Michaelis's book shall be referred to by footnotes. Mr. Michaelis, in "Looking Further Forward," used his quotations from Mr. Bellamy's book arbitrarily as illustrations of arguments, making a great show of statistics. His deductions will not bear scrutiny. The candid reader may judge, whether I have disproved his forced inferences from the same statistics.

LUDWIG A. GEISSLER.

Covington, La., January, 1891.

CHAPTER I.

Mr. Bellamy's "Looking Backward" having had such a wide circulation, especially since the cheapness of later editions has brought it within the reach of all, I shall restrict the synopsis of it to the shortest possible space.

Julian West, born in Boston in 1857, narrates his own story. He is well educated, in easy circumstances and of no particular profession. He is engaged to a beautiful and wealthy young lady, Miss Edith Bartlett, and intends to marry her as soon as his new house is built, the completion of which is delayed repeatedly by strikes.

In the meantime he lives in his old house, and as he suffers from insomnia, he had prepared there for a sleeping apartment a vault under the foundation of the house, undisturbed by the noise of the city and fire-proof, obtaining fresh air by mechanical means.

On May 30, 1887, after two sleepless nights, he made use of the services of a mesmerist, as he had done before when troubled with insomnia, giving orders to his servant, Sawyer, to awake him on the next morning at nine o'clock. The mesmerist, Dr. Pilsbury, left the city for New Orleans, and the house burned down that night, Sawyer probably perishing in the flames.

None of West's friends knew of the vault, the house was not rebuilt, and so he remained mesmerised and dormant, until in the year 2000, one Dr. Leete, on having the ground dug up for the foundation of a laboratory he intended to build, unearthed him and brought him to consciousness.

Mr. West learned in the course of a few days that Miss Edith Bartlett fourteen years after his supposed death had married, and that Dr. Leete's wife was her granddaughter.

He found the social and political conditions materially changed. The former competitive system had given way to one of general co-operation, the nation being producer and distributor, and similar arrangements in all civilised countries. He was quite overcome by the strangeness of his situation, but consoled by the compassion of Dr. Leete's daughter, Edith, who showed him how, in his moments of depression, he might find solace in most beautiful music, made audible in his bedroom by telephonic arrangements, to which a clockwork was attached, that could be set for any time of the twenty-four hours.

Dr. Leete gives him full explanation of the mode of living. Education is for all, male and female alike, the highest attainable until the age of twenty-one years, when they enter the industrial army. At the age of forty-five they are released from labour, and can only be summoned to work in exceptional cases of utmost necessity up to fifty-five. During the first three years of labour, they serve as recruits or apprentices in the auxiliary corps, being assigned to common labour, after which time they choose their trade or profession, which they enter in different grades, according to the record of their ability and behaviour during their apprenticeship. The honorary members (forty-five years of age and upward) of each trade or guild elect the general of the guild from among the colonels or superintendents. All trades are grouped in ten departments, and the honorary members of all allied trades or guilds belonging to one department elect its chief from among the generals of the guilds thus grouped as a department. The term of office of these ten department chiefs is five years. All honorary members of the nation elect the president from among the retired department chiefs for the term of five years. The outgoing president generally is elected by Congress to represent the nation for five years in the International Council, which regulates the mutual intercourse and commerce of the nations and their joint policy toward backward races. The generals appoint the officers under them, named colonels, or superintendents, captains or foremen, and lieutenants or assistant foremen, each from the rank next below, and the lieutenants from the first class of first grade of workers. The president, the chiefs and the generals, and several other high functionaries live in Washington; all state governments are abolished. The active members of the industrial army do not vote for their officers; any complaint is brought before a judge, who is appointed by the president for the term of five years, from among the men who have reached their forty-fifth year.

There is no money; but a credit card is given to every citizen alike for each successive year; cripples and others unable to work, as well as those exempt from work by their age, all receive the same. The work of the industrial army by division of labour, the united efforts of the nation's workers under one control, the use of machinery in every industrial branch increased continually by new inventions— all combine to make labour so productive, that it provides not only the necessities of life, but also the comforts and even luxuries for all. The hours of labour are short; lengthened for those guilds which are most desired; shortened for those where the labour is objectionable to many.

Each ward has a sample store, where purchasers choose what they want, and the amount is clipped out of their credit cards by the sample clerk. Cards are attached to the samples, giving full description and information of the qualities and price of the article. The orders are sent by pneumatic transmitters to the general warehouse, and the goods are thence conveyed to the purchaser's home without delay.

Large cooking houses furnish excellent meals. The inhabitants can have their meals there in elegant private rooms, or can have them brought home. They choose what dishes they please, and have the amount punched off their credit cards. Washing is done in great public laundries. They live in houses rented from the nation, having their own furniture.

Women likewise are members of the industrial army. They follow such employments as are perfectly adapted to their sex; their hours of labour are generally shorter than men's, their vacations more frequent. They serve the nation for the same term, and leave that service only temporarily when maternal duties call them. Thus, most women at one time or another serve industrially from five to fifteen years; those who have no children, the full term of twenty-four years. They have female officers and a female general-in-chief, who sits in the cabinet of the president, and who elects the female judges. Causes in which both parties are women, are determined by women judges, and where a man and a woman contend, a judge of each sex must consent to the verdict. They receive the same credit cards as the men, the nation likewise providing for the support of the children, who are dependent on their parents only for the offices of affection. Thus, with most of the household duties taken off them, women are very happy and independent. Marriages are for affection only, and the approval of the other sex acts as the strongest incentive on the young men to excel in their services to the nation. Laggards and the baser natures of men invariably form the only class of celibates, as the woman marrying one of these unfortunates has to defy public opinion. Hence, the human race is improved from generation to generation, the average life of individuals is longer than in the nineteenth century, and all look forward to the attainment of the forty-fifth year as the commencement of their happiest period, when, freed from labour, they can enjoy the rest of their lives entirely according to their inclinations—in travelling, study, pleasures of every kind, or ease and comfort at home.

There are no more lawyers, no courts, or jails, no sheriffs nor tax-collectors. Crimes or misdemeanors, since the abolition of money being very rare, are treated in hospitals as atavism.

The dread of want no more urges to great efforts. There are nobler motives and more effective. Among the various arrangements to arouse ambition is the investing with the red ribbon, which is the highest honour bestowed for excellence.

This is about the outline of the existing conditions of life, as Dr. Leete points them out to Julian West. The latter forms a warm attachment to Miss Edith Leete, which is reciprocated, and he is betrothed to the great-granddaughter of his former affianced. Anxious to find a place of utility in this to him a new world, he is installed as professor of the History of the Nineteenth Century.

On the day of his betrothal, it being Sunday, he

heard a sermon by telephone in Dr. Leete's house, in which the preacher strongly demonstrated the moral gap between the year 2000 and the nineteenth century. The state of depression Mr. West underwent in consequence of it, led to an interview with Edith Leete, his declaration and acceptance, as stated above. That night he dreamed that he was awakened in his vault by his man, Sawyer, and that all his experience of the last few days had been a dream. In this fancy he goes out, and, fresh from the recollection of the conversations he had with Dr. Leete after his resuscitation about the institutions and the life under the entirely different social and political conditions, he views the life of the nineteenth century with abhorrence. Finally to his great relief, he awakes again in the year 2000. His self-reproach for his inactivity toward amelioration of the existing evils, while he lived in the nineteenth century, found a merciful judge in Edith Leete, and here Mr. Bellamy's book ends.

In "Looking Further Forward," Mr. Michaelis commences with the first lecture held at Shawmut College by Mr. West. The latter explains the evils of the competitive system prevailing in the nineteenth century, and enthusiastically eulogises the communistic system of the twentieth. From the beginning of his lecture he noticed a man standing near the door, who remained after the students had left. This man introduced himself as Mr. Forest, West's predecessor as professor of nineteenth century history. He says that he had been deposed from this position and serves now as janitor, on account of his great preference to the competitive system, and for exposing the evils of the ruling system. In a number of conversations he attempts to prove that the ruling communistic system has bred favouritism and corruption to a degree vastly exceed-

ing that of the nineteenth century. He states that
all those who do not bribe the officers, and especially those who are adverse to the administration,
live a life of hell on earth, and are worse off than
slaves. He asserts that the only opposition the administration permits at election time is that of the
Radical Communists, whose demands are so atro-
cious and disgusting that the dread of them makes
the people submit to the tyranny of the administration. He accuses Dr. Leete of being a shrewd poli-
tician, a leader of tne administration party, enjoying more benefits than others, his daughter doing no
work, and the housework being done gratuitously by
the female auxiliary corps. All this makes a great
impression on Mr. West, who, knowing the existing
conditions only by Dr. Leete's words, finds himself
unable to disprove Mr. Forest's sophistic arguments.
His mind full with these conflicting emotions, according to Mr. Michaelis's narrative, he overhears at
Dr. Leete's house one Mr. Fest, a clever machinist,
captain in the industrial army and a RADICAL
LEADER. He had asked Miss Edith's hand and had
been rejected. He is furious, and uses insulting
language. Mr. West is informed that Fest, in his
childhood, lived in the neighbourhood and used to
play with Edith. Some more conversation with Mr.
Forest ensues, and then follows the outbreak of the
Radicals. A dirty, ruffianly crowd, led by Fest,
burst into Dr. Leete's house. Forest rushes into the
room, and tries to save Dr. Leete, in the attempt of
which he is stabbed to death. West is overpowered
and bound, to be dumped, as Mr. Fest expressed it,
in Boston harbour. Fest, wielding an axe, splits
open Dr. Leete's head, then seizing the lifeless body
of the fainted Edith, he calls on his ruffian accom-
plices to kill every friend of the administration. In
his frantic efforts to free himself from his bonds,

Mr. West finally awakes in his vault on May 31, 1887, a physician and his man, Sawyer, by his side. Thinking over all the experiences he has undergone, he concludes that all was a dream, and blesses the nineteenth century.

So far Mr. Michaelis, in "Looking Further Forward." In the next chapter Mr. Julian West will tell his own story.

CHAPTER II.

I opened my eyes; they rested on the clock before me, which Edith had put there, knowing that I had been accustomed to it. It wanted five minutes to eight. I was puzzled. Gradually recollections came back. Surely this was my room in Dr. Leete's house, and yet it seemed but a short time that I awoke in my own vault, after having passed through such terrible scenes in my dream.

Now, which was real? Was this awakening in my room in Dr. Leete's house a dream, or the awakening in my vault? Was this the nineteenth century or the twentieth? And if the latter, was the terrible experience with Fest and the Radicals a dream or reality? My head began to swim; I felt intensely miserable; worse than when I returned that morning from my early walk. Then the sense of loneliness overpowered me at finding all my tender ties of friends and humanity severed, and realised that in all that bustling city I was alone, with not a tie to bind me to a mortal being. But oh, how vastly more dreadful were now my sufferings! I felt a whirling and hammering sensation in my brain. A chill, an icy horror, crept over me. I felt that I was going mad.

At that moment soft notes floated through the room. Sweet, intensely sweet, sounded "Annie Laurie," executed by a violin and flute. Edith, always mindful of my comforts, had set the telephonic arrangement for eight o'clock. The effect on me was magical. An intense longing, coupled with sadness, seized me. The whirling in my brain, the mingling and wrangling of confused ideas, stopped. All settled into one thought: "Edith." Tears came to my eyes; my brain was saved.

There I lay, still sad, but calm, confiding, as in my childhood I had felt myself safe in my mother's arms.

"I'd lay me doon and dee" breathed through the air, dissolving, melting away, that I still heard it, mentally, after the last note had sounded.

Then, majestically and triumphant, the "Song of the Red Ribbon," executed by a full orchestra, stirred my blood. That masterpiece of twentieth century composition, that grand utterance of sublimest joy and consciousness of victory, aroused me, lifted the depression off my soul and spiritually intoxicated me.

I rose and dressed. The music ceased, and the depression came back on me. But my mind was calm. I could reason now; I could clearly discern reality and dream.

Oh yes! It was yesterday that Mr. Forest had given me such a sickening description of the evil effects of twentieth century's communism, of favouritism and corruption, that made my heart sink within me, that shattered the enthusiastic pictures of the present generation's happiness which Dr. Leete's glowing description had conjured before me. Yes, I remember now, how I went home depressed and sick at heart, and, feigning headache, sought my room. Then I went to bed. All this was reality.

And the conflicting statements of Dr. Leete and Mr. Forest, the strangeness of my reawakening, that seeming double life, impressions and experiences of my former life—all these combined to create that terrible dream. Fest? No, I never saw him, except in my dream; I only heard his name mentioned by Mr. Forest.

Oh yes! Thank heaven, that brutal conduct of Fest, his murder of Dr. Leete and Forest, his kidnapping of Edith, his gang tying and gagging me —all this was but a dream. But there still remained the doubts created by Mr. Forest's arguments. I needed a long conversation with Dr. Leete, a thorough explanation; but first I had to see Edith.

I left the room, and, passing through the hall, I found Edith sitting near the open door in the same room where once before she had consoled me.

"Oh, Mr. West!—Julian!" she exclaimed, as she read in my face the havoc made by the storm of conflicting passions and agonies. She rose quickly, but I gently forced her down again; and, seating myself at her feet, my head resting against her, my hands clinging to hers, a feeling of rest came over me. Then I looked up and feasted my eyes on the tender expressions of mingled love and pity in her sweet face, and then I made a full confession.

With her rosy fingers she gently stroked the hair back from my forehead. "I noticed yesterday evening that something was wrong," she said. "I was waiting here for you, to be in time to exorcise the clouds from your overburdened mind. Oh! Why did you not speak last night and save yourself the agonies that you must have suffered? I can well understand it. The singular idiosyncrasy of Mr. Forest was quite amusing thus far; but common decency should teach him to give you time to become accustomed to our institutions and to understand them, not from hearsay merely, but from your own observation and experience, before he tries to argue with you on them. And so," she added smiling, " Mr. Forest thinks that neither my mother nor I do any housework, or maybe that I don't do any work at all? *Oh, I daresay, his constant study of nineteenth century history has so far blinded his knowledge of the twentieth century that he thinks we are supported all three by my father's credit card. My dear Julian, there is not so much housework to be done, since washing and cooking no more belong to household duties, and this my mother and I do alternately in a very short time. Oh, you will be surprised when you see the machines and contrivances we have for that purpose, such as our great-grandmothers never dreamt of. Now, did it not strike you that you never saw me during breakfast and dinner time? Where do you think that I am during that time? There are so many things new to you that I had no chance to tell you yet. I am at my work in the ramie spinning mill. It is only about three months that my duties in the auxiliary corps were ended, and I choose that employment because I have a particular liking for it. It leaves me plenty of leisure time, only three hours consummating a day's work, with two vacations in the year. Any extra housework we have done by members of the auxiliary corps, but we pay for it by having the amount clipped off from our three credit cards."

"Four," I said, pressing to my heart the sweet creature who had plighted her troth to me; "four, since I am allowed a credit card, too, in this happy land."

"Four be it then, Mr. Professor," and her fresh red lips yielded to the kiss I imprinted on them in

---

* Page 73, "Looking Further Forward."

my ecstasy. I was happy beyond measure. Of course, I never had doubted Edith's integrity, but Forest's remarks had indicated an abuse of power from Dr. Leete's side. And now I sincerely hoped that he could as easily blow off all the other accusations against him and against the ruling system.

No lecture was to be held this day, and I was at full leisure for a long talk with Dr. Leete.

We were sitting in the library after breakfast, and, when our cigars were lit, I unburdened my mind to him.

"I am glad," he said, with his usual kindness, "that you confide to me the doubts and troubles created by the false arguments and mis-statements of Mr. Forest. He is a very good man and a noble soul; but he is one of those, fortunately very rare, specimens of humanity who, over their studies of the past, forget entirely to understand the present. He studied so deeply the history of the nineteenth century that he formed for himself a theory, and sees and understands nothing but that, notwithstanding that the facts disprove it, as some members of the nineteenth and former centuries loved to look still further back into antiquity for the Golden Age. Of course, his obstinate mis-statements disqualified him for the continuation of his task. He had the option to choose his future occupation; he preferred to be janitor where he had lectured before, as any kind of labour is honourable with us, and it was granted him. To us, who know better, his arguments are harmless; but you, having seen so little of our life yet, must naturally be startled by them. Now, to begin : what did he tell you about the Radicals in general, and about Mr. Fest particularly? It must have been the most absurd misrepresentation to cause such a terrible dream."

"He says that the Radicals are denouncing religion, marriage, separate housekeeping and the limited amount of property people are permitted to own;* that they desire us to live together in lodging houses accommodating thousands of people,† because it would be cheaper to lodge thousands under one roof;‡ that they say, if marriage was abolished, the passing alliances of men and women would produce better children, who would be brought up in large nurseries, so that the mothers could attend all day to their work in the industrial army.§ He further says that they advocate to live together like rabbits,‖ and dwelling on the particulars of such a system in a manner too beastly to mention,¶ he asserts that the administration permits them to advocate their ideas before election to scare the people into submission."**

Dr. Leete shook his head: "Why, the man is going from bad to worse. All this exists only in his confused brain. As for religion, that is entirely private matter with us,†† and regarding such sexual aberrations, just use your common sense, Mr. West! Do you think it probable, that ladies and gentlemen, who received the highest attainable education up to twenty-one years—who have plenty leisure time and the means to enjoy it—who mix with none but equally polished and refined people—would advocate such principles? And can you imagine among a nation of thus highly cultured men and women a spiritless, humble mass of people that can

---

* Page 57, "Looking Further Forward."
† Page 71, "Looking Forward."
‡ Page 75, "Looking Forward."
§ Page 76, "Looking Forward."
‖ Page 71, "Looking Further Forward."
¶ Pages 77 to 78, "Looking Forward."
** Page 58. "Looking Forward."
†† Pages 272 and 273, "Looking Backward."

be scared into submission? The majority of our people live in private houses as we do, larger or smaller, according to the number of their family members. But there are some who club together and rent immense hotels, where they can enjoy the privacy of their own elegantly furnished bed-rooms or the grand parlours and halls for society, *ad libitum*. Mr. Fest lives in one of those phalansteries by his own preference, it being the tendency of our institutions, after exacting a certain very limited amount of labour out of every person for a fixed period, to let every one follow his or her individual taste in spending the very ample income. Mr. Fest is called a Radical, but the object of his endeavours is entirely legitimate, and he and those of the same mind certainly are not a political party in the sense of the nineteenth century. I have informed you that the lieutenants, captains and colonels of the industrial army are appointed by the generals of the guild. Now, Mr. Fest and numerous others, advocate to have them elected by the privates of the industrial army out of the first class of highest grade. The old system suited very well, but I think it's worth the trial, and at the next voting done by us exempt members, I, for my part, shall be in favour of trying it first with the lieutenants. If such should prove superior, then we can always extend it to the captains. Most probably Mr. Forest, whose mind lives continually in the nineteenth century, has mixed up all this in his confused brain, and imagines all sorts of horrors to be dreaded from the very well-meaning and deserving Radicals. Mr. Fest is a machinist of great ability; otherwise he would not be captain at less than thirty years of age, and he has the best chances to be promoted to colonel as soon as there is a vacancy. You see by that how disinterested his motives are, as he has nothing to gain by such a change. It really is a pity to see a man of Mr. Forest's mental powers to be so much of a monomaniac that he construes in his own mind quite a detestable character and clothes it with such an exemplary young man. I noticed in your short sketch of Mr. Forest's remarks some hints about an administration party. We will discuss that some other time. I merely wish you to use your own judgment. If there were an administration party unrestrainedly practising favouritism, as Mr. Forest represents it, do you think it consistent with the weakest common sense that they would appoint to and keep in such a position a man who is, according to Mr. Forest, their most deadly enemy? And now picture yourself a young man who, up to twenty-one years, has received the highest attainable education, who since then has arrived at such perfection, practically and scientifically, in the most important and most difficult of trades, that he holds a high position of the greatest responsibility, even while he is in his twenties yet—picture all this, and compare with it the ruffian Mr. Forest would have you believe him to be! He is very young yet. His parents formerly lived next door, and, when he was a boy, he used to play with Edith.* *From that you may guess his age.* You shall see him yourself, and, no doubt, you will soon be great friends."

I must say that while Dr. Leete had been speaking in such a calm, kind and convincing manner, I felt a load moving off my heart; but his last remarks brought back some feeling of uneasiness, and I could not help saying: "There is something at least in which Mr. Forest spoke the truth."

---

* Page 68, "Looking Further Forward."

"Oh yes," said the doctor; "and even to-day they are fast friends. Oh, you need have no apprehension," he added, smiling; "he never will be a rival to you. His affection lies in a different quarter altogether. It is the great misfortune of his life. He deeply loves a very pretty young lady and a particular friend of Edith but his love is not returned."

I heaved a sigh of relief, but a revulsion of feelings following immediately, I said, with a sigh of pity, "Poor fellow!"

"Let me see," said Dr. Leete after short reflection: "To-night we have the monthly reunion in my club, the Club of the Professionals of this city, which, of course, you too will join. I can promise you quite a lively time. There will be private theatricals, very good novelties, written for the occasion by some of our own members, humorous lectures dancing, exquisite telephonic concerts, and so on. You will meet there lots of interesting people, and by their conversation get accustomed to our institutions quicker than at home. I'll send an invitation to Mr. Fest. You may be sure that he will accept it, for he knows that his lady love will be there, being the daughter of an old colleague of mine, and he has not given up hope to win her over yet. What do you think of that?"

"I shall be delighted," I said.

"Now," the doctor added, "if I understood you aright, Mr. Forest said something about the laboratory I intend to build."

"So he did. He said your building a laboratory for yourself is entirely against the intentions and spirit of our institutions. There is a very good laboratory in the basement of the college, and you certainly would be welcome to experiment there at your pleasure. It is an expensive affair, for which the credit cards of ten men would not pay; and you assume an exceptional position, which not only savours of favouritism, but also involves an indiscreet abuse of power."*

Dr. Leete laughed. "The very fact that Mr. Forest is permitted to utter such calumnies proves that there is no abuse of power, in treating a troublesome crank at least. There certainly is a very good laboratory in the basement, not of the college, but of a large outhouse at the further end of the college grounds, and I use it occasionally for some experiments when I can do so without disturbance. But you will understand that I *can* use it *only* occasionally; besides, I have an object before me. I will tell you in confidence that I made a great discovery, and I am working away at an invention which shall make that discovery very useful to mankind. A great deal of study and a number of experiments are needed yet before I can hope to succeed. You see, I am striving for the red ribbon in my old days. Now, for such labours I need my own laboratory. But what is it? Most of the instruments and material I have already, and for that little building? Poor man! To make such wild statements. The credit cards of ten men, indeed! Just imagine, a tiny brick building with brick floor, chimney, and a few other contrivances, to cost the credit cards of ten men, to cost the means for comfortable and even luxurious living for ten men in one year! Did you ever hear anything so ridiculous?"

I could not help laughing.

He continued: "The surplus of our three credit cards will pay for the first start. The rest will be completed next year."

---

* Pages 50 and 51, "Looking Further Forward."

I felt rather serious after this. "All this is so plain and so logical," I said, "that I feel ashamed of not having used the same arguments myself."

"You could not," said Dr. Leete reassuring. "All our institutions are new to you yet. Thus far you only heard my praise of them, followed by Mr. Forest's utter condemnation. Now, you shall judge for yourself. In a few weeks the short vacation begins. I would advise you during that time to study the life of our farmers on the farms, and to hear from their own lips what they have to say. And thus let it be with all the assertions of Mr. Forest! See hear, and judge for yourself!"

I shook hands with the doctor and thanked him heartily. I felt fresh and buoyant again.

That afternoon Edith led me into the mysteries of dancing in the twentieth century. She certainly was a very pleasant teacher, and the time of instruction, which lasted nearly two hours, was spent in a very gratifying manner. She finally agreed that I would do very well in the evening.

CHAPTER III.

The club house of the professionals was a splendid, palatial building, some eight or nine squares distant from Dr. Leete's house. The grand hall, gorgeously decorated, was lighted brilliantly. A small stage with exquisitely painted curtain filled the background, with numerous dressing rooms on both sides. There was no place for an orchestra. The parquette contained very comfortable seats, four aisles passing between them toward the stage, and a broad walk leading all around. A row of boxes, very pleasantly fitted up, extended around the hall one story higher. A dozen wide doors, opening to the outside, enabled the hall to be cleared in less than a minute in case of an accident; the same arrangements were made on the gallery, which contained the boxes. All these exits led through various rooms to the corridors and vestibules, from which again the streets could be reached without delay. The rooms around the hall were of different sizes. There were refreshment rooms of large dimensions for those who preferred to enjoy the pleasures of general society; there were smaller ones for a few intimate friends and private families; there were smoking rooms for gentlemen and parlours exclusively for ladies.

As our party entered the vestibule we were accosted by a pleasant gentleman of Dr. Leete's age, whom he introduced to me as Dr. Moore. The latter in turn presented to me his wife, his two daughters, Mary and Ellen, and his son, Richard, a sprightly young man of about nineteen years. Miss Mary, who at once took possession of Edith, seemed about her age, while Miss Ellen appeared no more than about twenty-one. Dr. Leete likewise introduced to me three or four gentlemen and two ladies of the reception committee. Then, finding that most boxes were vacant yet, it was decided that we all should repair to box No. 11, one of the larger ones. Dr. Leete asked the chairman of the reception committee to direct Captain Fest to our box.

"Certainly," he said, with a bow, and our party was on the point of moving, when Miss Mary Moore stepped up to him. "Please, direct Mr. Uriah Brown likewise to our box," she said.

"Whom, Miss Moore?" exclaimed the gentleman in surprise.

At that moment I noticed that Edith's hand trembled, and her pretty nose and lips were drawn up just a little. I also noticed Miss Ellen Moore to blush, her brother to frown, and everybody around to look slightly embarrassed. I noticed all this at a glance, then I looked at Miss Mary again. She really was a picture. A rich pink spread over her generally pale face, covering even her forehead and the neck behind her ear; her delicate nostrils dilated, her gray eyes almost looked black, shedding darts of fire.

"Mr. Uriah Brown," she repeated, with a voice clear and hard like marbles dropped on a smooth slate. "Mr. Uriah Brown, second class, third grade of the Street Cleaning Fraternity."

The gentleman by this time had mastered his surprise. He bowed politely, and we moved on to our box. I stayed a little behind to get an explanation of all this. Leaning on my arm, as we walked on slowly, Edith whispered hurriedly: "Oh, I'm so sorry that we took a box together with the Moores. You must know, Mr. Fest loves Mary with all his fervour, and as my father had invited him, I thought this a fine chance of bringing them together. She is a great friend of mine. She is a splendid creature, and so clever. We always have been together at school, and we chose the same trade when we had served our time in the auxiliary corps. I entered in the first class of the third grade, but expect to get into the second grade at the next regrading. Mary, however, got into the second grade at once. How well Mr. Fest would be suited to her! Just imagine! Only twenty-nine years old and already captain in the Machinist Guild, the most important of all. And that perverse creature cannot appreciate him in the least. No! She just adores that insignificant Uriah Brown, a man who lost his trade. Six years ago he had entered the Machinist Guild in the second grade, rose to the first grade in the following year, and gave promise of just such rapid rise as Mr. Fest, when suddenly a change came over him. He grew listless and inattentive, and occasionally spoiled his work. He was reduced at every regrading, and finally, being fit for nothing else, he had to join the street cleaners. And even there he plays a sorry figure. He is in the second class of the third grade. And such a man she prefers to Mr. Fest. She takes his part against her family and all her friends. You saw yourself an evidence of her interest in him. She says he works at an invention in his leisure hours. And now we will have both suitors with her in the same box. It is very annoying, and I am really sorry for Mr. Fest."

So was I, but had no chance to say so, as we entered the box at that moment. And yet, strong as was the compassion which I felt for Mr. Fest, I could not help being elated to notice how Edith was intent on match-making for him. If any trace of jealous feeling would have lingered in my breast, that would have obliterated it.

The box was very large. The two elder couples, in lively conversation, took their seats, while the three young Moores stood at the entrance yet. Ellen and Richard must have passed some not very flattering remarks about Uriah Brown, for Miss Moore, in the same striking attitude she had assumed in the vestibule, said just then: "You will ask his pardon on your knees when he wears the red ribbon."

We went to the front; I looked around. The parquette was more than half filled already, while in the boxes the people were just coming in. A constant humming indicated that a lively conversation was going on all around, and salutations were exchanged between parquette and boxes. Just as we were seated, Mr. Uriah Brown entered. He was a tall, raw-boned man, with a listless expression in his face. His dress, although faultlessly clean, hung loosely on him. Bowing stiffly all around, at length his eyes rested on Mary Moore. There was an immediate change in his expression, his face seemed to light up. Miss Mary shook hands with him warmly, and then introduced him to me. He looked at me with a curious expression, bowed, and sat down by the side of the young lady. They conversed immediately in an undertone about movements and springs and wheels and other mechanical implements.

And now Mr. Fest entered. A fine looking young man, with a splendid physique, firm expression and elegant manners. A frown hung menacingly on his brow for one moment when he saw Uriah Brown, but it passed off directly, and warmly he shook hands with my host, who had risen to greet him. How different he was to the Fest in my horrid dream! Dr. Leete introduced us. After paying homage to Mrs. Leete and exchanging a few words with Dr. Moore, and a salutation to the others, Mr. Fest sat down by my side.

At that moment a clear bell sounded, announcing the beginning. All was hushed. The first piece on the programme was the overture to the modern grand opera, "Reňa." What ravishing harmony! How the wonderfully rich sounds swelled and filled the hall! And that adagio! Like zephyrs breathing gently amid roses! And to think that in numerous places all over this great city they enjoy the same music at the same time! Edith told me that all concerts in club houses are given by telephonic arrangements. There is but one opera house in Boston, but of such dimensions that it can hold forty thousand people. She says that the acoustic arrangement is unexceptional, and that about two hundred musicians of the first grade form the orchestra. We decided to go there after a few days.

The curtain rose, and a highly humorous lecture by Mr. Beard, a renowned painter, was followed by a comedy, well written and as well executed. After a succession of musical pieces and other entertainments the bell tinkled again, and I noticed that all the spectators in the parquette rose and leisurely walked out in all directions. Edith smiled and said I soon would have another surprise. Then again a bell struck, and the whole parquette, seats and all, ascended slowly. Slowly and steadily it came up, passed the boxes until it reached the top, where it fitted exactly. The reverse side of it was beautifully painted, and thus it formed a new ceiling, while the new floor was polished and splendidly adapted for dancing. The tune of the opening dance sounded, and from every side young ladies and gentlemen swarmed into the hall. Richard had left the box as soon as the first chords struck, and appeared now below, a pretty young damsel on his arm.

All this time poor Mr. Fest must have suffered tortures. Now and then he had thrown a side glance at Miss Moore, who never noticed him, being wholly absorbed in Mr. Uriah Brown. Miss Ellen had watched the unrequited lover with pity and compassion, and had done her best to divert his mind, but she met with but poor result. Now Miss Moore rose, and, taking Mr. Brown's arm, she left the box with him, and soon afterward they could be seen below, sauntering about. Edith looked at Mr. Fest and then at me. I understood her meaning and asked her for a dance. She rose, laid her arm into mine and asked Mr. Fest to join us with Ellen. He blushed. He looked at Edith quite confusedly, like a person awaking suddenly from an evil dream.

Then he rose; he was himself again directly. Politely he offered his arm to Ellen, and we joined the dancers together.

After an hour or so our little party met again in one of the smaller refreshment rooms for supper. We were a pretty lively party, and even Mr. Fest did his best to appear cheerful. If he did not feel so, it certainly was not Ellen's fault. She did her best to make him forget her sister. Even Mr. Brown, who had at first been eating silently, afterward joined the conversation, and when Dr. Leete in his kind manner asked him about his invention, he grew quite eloquent. His listless manner was changed, his eyes shone, and he spoke with fervour.

"We pride ourselves so much on our civilisation," he said. "What is there to be proud of? True, we have machines for almost any kind of performance, and even I, second-class, third-grade worker of the Street Cleaning Fraternity, need not wield the broom, as they did a hundred years ago, but can sit on my machine, which is the slave to do the labour for us." His eyes darted sparks of fire as he said so and Miss Moore looked at him with enthusiasm. "But," he resumed, "where is the progress in the power we have subjugated for our labours? What lights our streets and houses, cooks our meals, warms our rooms, sets all our machines in motion? Electricity. Where did we get the knowledge of subjugating that giant to serve our demands? Did we discover it? Did we invent the process? No, we inherited it from the last century. We merely improved on it. Our ancestors could well be proud of it; for them it was an innovation, a great progress; it was the child of their time. But we, during a whole century have found nothing better; we still use that clumsy wasteful power, dangerous in the highest degree in spite of all our improvements

Looking Beyond. 31

and safety-guards. Where do all these different powers, that man has employed already, originate? Do they not all come from the sun? The rays of the sun striking our earth give us light and warmth, and keep up that constant circulation from the ocean to the clouds, from them through the hearts of the mountains in brooks and rivers to the ocean again. Why not seize that power in its origin, concentrate and condense it, and have an unerring and constant slave to human will and human energy?"

It was a splendid sight to look at Miss Moore. She was radiant with enthusiasm, when Uriah Brown spoke thus.

"Then you mean to say," asked Dr. Moore, with a mocking smile, "that you aim at condensing the rays of the sun?"

"I mean to say no more on the subject," said Mr. Brown, rising. "My invention is my own, and nobody will be the wiser of it until I can bring it before the public as a final success, I will not share the red ribbon with anyone. And now, ladies and gentlemen, I have to depart. My task, as second-class, third-grade street cleaner, begins shortly."

With a light bow he left the room, accompanied by Miss Moore.

"I am afraid he is chasing after some wild chimera," said Dr. Moore.

"Perhaps so," mused Dr. Leete. And yet who can tell? His general remarks give me no hints whatever, but that he is labouring on a new motor. He certainly shows no lack of energy for his hobby, and no doubt he has knowledge."

"That he has," said Mr. Fest. "Before this listlessness came on him, he was the best machinist practically in this city, and his theoretical knowledge of natural philosophy was immense. I suppose, it was brooding over this invention that caused the sudden change in him, the want of attention to his task."

Miss Moore entered the room again.

"This case illustrates strikingly the difference between this century and the nineteenth," I added. "Then, a man in such condition would have been compelled to work long hours for a mere pittance. His energy would have been worn off, or his bodily strength wasted. He would most probably have found a premature death as a drunkard, vagrant or suicide; and even if the power of his genius would have been so great as to overcome with the greatest personal sacrifices all obstacles, it could have been only to see at the last moments the fruits of his brain racking, and the honour, too, reaped by an impostor with means. Now, it is different. The man losing his grade, and even his trade, whatever he does, works but a portion of the day, enjoys all the necessities and comforts of life, and his mind is not burdened with care for them. He has ample spare time to work out the design which the sparks of genius awaken in his brain, though it should take the whole period of his life. He can even marry and enjoy the company of his family in ease and comfort."

Dr. Leete then spoke of the strange idiosyncrasy of Mr. Forest. Dr. Moore informed us that Mr. Yale, the professor of statistics, volunteered to have a public discussion with Mr. Forest, and to "smash" all his nonsensical theories into splinters.

"I am glad of that," I said. "I shall certainly not miss this opportunity. My ears are yet tingling with his description of the miserable condition caused by the present system, and yet I see nothing but comfort around me. He says that those members of the industrial army who have drawn down upon themselves the ire of the officers of the administration, or whose voting relatives are on the opposition side—such members lead a life that may be termed as twenty-four years of hell on earth.* He also asserts, there is an established favouritism of the officers to their friends and relatives, to the extent that they pass an easy time with best records during the three years of apprenticeship, enter at once the first class of first grade in the guild they have chosen, and are thus immediately appointed to lieutenancy, whence they may run up to the higher honours in a few years.† Also that occasional presents of wine and cigars may secure the friendship of some of the officers."

"Why, that is outrageous," exclaimed Mr. Fest, "And do you believe that?"

"He certainly made it appear very feasible to me. I sincerely hope that it is not true."

"To begin with the last, the most petty of these slanders, let me point out to you a parallel, Mr. West. Imagine you live again in the nineteenth century! Then imagine a body of men, all having received college and university education! Imagine, then, furthermore, all to be in such conditions of life that they can procure all necessities and comforts and even some luxuries as long as they live! Their duty calls on them during twenty-four years of their life for a certain task that will occupy a few hours a day. What would you have called these men?"

"Why gentlemen, of course," I said.

"Very good," he continued. "Now, one of these gentlemen is assigned to direct the task required of them. Do you think it probable that some of such highly-educated gentlemen, all equal, all without care for their subsistence, would be mean enough

---

* Page 43, "Looking Further Forward."
† Page 40, "Looking Further Forward."

to bribe their lieutenant, so that they might shirk some of their light and short-timed duty? And do you think the highly-educated gentleman directing their tasks, whose income permits him to have as many cigars and as much wine as he likes, would be capable of being bribed with some wine and a few cigars?"

"Of course not," I said. "Why, that's simply ridiculous."

"Well, and that's just how our people stand to-day. Mr. Forest's study of the nineteenth century must have been so intense that he imagines the same conditions to exist yet as they did then with what they called working men. I have read something about the nineteenth century, too, and then such conditions were quite natural. Of course, a man who works hard from morning till night, who had no chance of any decent education, who barely received in return for such labour the means of keeping himself and family from starvation, with no security for the future—such a man might sacrifice even something of his pittance for a bribe, and the taskmaster, with no better education and the same insecurity, might be capable of receiving petty bribes. And as to the members of the industrial army leading a life of hell on earth, if they happen to be on bad standing with the officers, or if their voting relatives should be on the opposite side, always keep in mind that the education and long intellectual training we receive, all alike, plants firmly in our hearts a sense of honour and self-respect which renders men incapable of ever being enslaved! Remember also that during the twenty-four years of work our tasks are light and hours of labour short, our leisure and decent living keeping up mental and bodily vigour, so that none of us are in a condition to lessen the sense of honour and self-respect! Do you really think it possible that such a body of men would submit to such tyranny and injustice?"

"No, certainly not," I exclaimed, quite delighted. "That's entirely out of the question. Why, even in the nineteenth century, among those that had been raised in factory towns or near mines, who, yet in their childhood, had to labour for their subsistence, with no knowledge but their task, cowering before the frown of their overseer, brow-beaten and cuffed, systematically trained for slavery—even among those were men who held up their self-respect, who scorned to crouch before their lords. What Mr. Forest asserts is simply impossible."

"The same it is with Forest's assertion of favouritism practised by the officers. I have to remind you again of the fact that all our men are highly educated. Don't you think a body of such men, working together, should be efficient to know who is entitled to promotion, and who not? Is it not self-evident that wholesale favouritism, as suggested, or rather asserted, by Mr. Forest, would create such a storm of indignation as to oust the corrupt parties practising it? Still, for the very reason that we all have received the highest attainable intellectual training, the members of the industrial army themselves are good judges of the efficiency to promotion among their comrades, and it seems to me but right that they should themselves elect their lieutenants out of the first class, first grade, and the captains among the lieutenants, while the right of electing the generals and chiefs might still be reserved to the exempt members solely as heretofore. There is a strong movement on foot to that effect, which some call a radical movement, and I am active in that cause."

"And I am willing to give it a trial with the lieutenants for a beginning," said Dr. Leete. "I shall vote in favour of it at the next Congress."

"So will I," added Dr. Moore.

After listening to the performance of a beautiful symphony, our party broke up for the night.

CHAPTER IV.

Two days later I was married to Edith Leete. The procedure is very simple. The loving couple, generally accompanied by the parents and a few friends, call on the judge nearest their new home, and enter their names into a book of records kept there. Those who belong to some religious community are wedded again by their minister or priest, but that is entirely optional. We had just entered our names, when Mary Moore came up with Uriah Brown for the same purpose. They were alone. The poor girl had to brave the disapproval of her whole family and all her friends, who thought it an outrage that a woman, standing so high in the guild, should marry a man who not only had lost his former high grade, but even his trade, and now belonged to the lowest grade of common labourers. Her swollen eyes indicated that she felt severely the rupture with her family and the sneers and taunts of her friends, but she remained firm. Her great love for Uriah Brown, and her staunch belief in his genius, which would triumph finally, bore her through the ordeal. Edith, too, was incensed against her for breaking with what might be called the spirit of the age—that is, to scorn the idea of marrying a laggard. She likewise felt greatly disappointed to have failed in matchmaking, having set her heart on seeing Fest and

Mary Moore united in wedlock. Still, her friendship and great pity overcame these ill-feelings. She embraced and kissed Mary, added her name as witness to the signature of the bride and groom, and prevailed on me to do the same. Nor did her charity end there. As I found out afterward, she took her part against the taunts of Mary's former friends to such an extent that some of the odium even fell on her.

My vacation setting in shortly afterward, and Edith exchanging hers with one of her co-workers, whose two weeks' vacation occurred at the same time, we started on our bridal tour.

Aeronautics have improved greatly since the nineteenth century, yet they are far from perfection. . . . . The electric railroads, like electric water traffic, have come to such perfection, that wonderful speed, comfort and safety are united.

Our first destination was a lovely spot at the foot of the Catskill mountains, near the Hudson river, where I enjoyed for a week in solitude the company of my beloved wife.

That time passed away like a blissful dream; a letter from Dr. Leete, however, aroused us to the fact that I had an object before me.

A few hours' ride brought us into the heart of the Adirondack mountains. We had a beautiful view as we left the extensive depot. To the right of us a grand waterfall was utilised to create the electric power used in the numerous works around. These electric works were adjoined by an immense sawmill, where everything, even the handling of the logs, as well as of the sawn lumber, was done by machinery. Planing mill, paper mill and other works were near by. Right before us the broad valley, surrounded by heavily timbered hills, was occupied by quite a little city. Comfortable one and two storey houses lined the streets, intersecting at right angles, all having little flower gardens in the rear. The centre of this town formed an immense square, with fine shade trees, lawns, walks and beautiful flower patches, and some magnificent palatial buildings. The largest one of these edifices was the hotel, with immense kitchen arrangements in the basement, grand dining halls, libraries, etc., on the first floor, and in the higher stories a number of nicely furnished bedrooms for those unmarried members of the industrial army who had no family connections, and for the use of occasional visitors to the place. Other imposing structures were the school house and the warehouse; there also were the theatre and a few more public buildings. The depot being on elevated ground, the whole presented a delightful picture.

After partaking of a sumptuous dinner, we spent the rest of the day in examining the different arrangements, which were all a marvel to me. I learned that not only the Adirondacks, but all mountain chains of North America, were under scientific treatment, the land being divided into sections, which were replanted immediately after the lumber was taken off. Rail tracks passed through the woods in various directions, the working force and needed machinery being always conveyed to and from the place for labour by electric cars and vans, four hours being the assigned time for each set of men. Women were employed in the public laundry, in the cooking establishment, and in the paper mill, where wood pulp was used up by a new process. We had a trip on one of these trains that conveyed a new labour force to the place of work, bringing back those who were relieved. It was highly interesting to me to see labour, that used to exert the utmost strength of man, performed almost playfully and in an incredibly short time, by machinery. A curiously constructed ring was placed around the tree and connected with the electric wire—a whizzing sound—and the tree fell. By the same process the trees were cut up into saw-logs of the required length. Another machine loaded the trucks with logs, and when there was a sufficient number of trucks thus loaded, the train started off for the mill. All the labour required was connecting and disconnecting the various implements and machinery with the electric current. Still constant attention was necessary.

Half an hour's walk brought us back to the next section, where the woods had been cleared the week previous. Here another force was at work. The sound of constant detonations led us to a place where the stumps were annihilated by explosives ignited by electric sparks. Further on an electric monster plough was at work. After passing this, we saw a machine in action, boring big holes in the ground, and a set of men right behind the machine, busy in planting young trees. I have been informed that since this system of clearing and replanting by sections had been introduced in the forests, inundations, as well as occasional droughts, which did so much damage in the latter part of the nineteenth century, are almost unknown.

The gentleman who had been our cicerone since we had left the depot was a young man of about thirty years, whose acquaintance we made while we were at dinner. He had introduced himself as Mr. Ben Rouleaix, second grade worker. He had that morning been employed planting trees and as one set of men worked four hours in the morning, the other set four hours in the afternoon, he was at liberty. Of course; they all had read about my wonderful resuscitation, and it had been discussed at great length among them; therefore, it was no news to him. Still the gentlemanly tact with which he mastered his surprise, when I told him who I was, seemed to me quite admirable. While we were watching the planting of the trees, our conversation drifted on Mr. Forest's queer theories, of which he had read in the paper.

"It seems to me," he said, "that Mr. Forest's theories are not consistent with his actions. While he denounces our present civilisation, he enjoys all the benefits of it. We can boast here of a man whose consistency in that respect cannot be denied. It is a very strange case of atavism. The man I'm alluding to is now about seventy years old. He is generally called Old Pete. At the age of twenty-one, when his labours in the industrial army should have commenced, he refused to work. It was represented to him that society thus far had educated, fed and clothed him, and that now it would be his duty to return to society these benefits by his labour. He answered that he had not asked for these benefits —they were forced on him—therefore, he owed nothing to society. On being reminded that the comparatively slight task required of him for twenty-four years only would sustain him in ease and comfort for the rest of his life, he said that he could live without it. He knew how his grandfather used to live in the woods, and he would do the same. He didn't care how hard he worked for himself, but he would never work under another man's orders for society. No, not one minute. He was placed under medical treatment in the hospital, but he denounced that as tyranny. His atavism was incurable. He demanded his liberty, and so he was permitted to live outside the pale of society, as long as he in no wise would encroach on it. The general impression was that the misery of his condition would soon bring him back to civilisation. But if he was a crank, he certainly was a consistent one. Do you see yonder peak? It is very steep, its wood growth is virgin. There is a plateau of about an acre's dimensions on the top of it, where he has built a little room out of young trees, and something attached to it, made of clay, which he calls a chimney. There he lives in quite a savage state, boasting to enjoy the liberty of the nineteenth century, raising some kinds of vegetables with the utmost labour, gathering mushrooms and herbs in the woods. When he first moved up there, nobody cared for him any more. He was considered non-existent, the more so, as he never showed himself. But our present generation of young people often take a stroll up there for curiosity. They generally take some provisions along and leave them there. Not only old age, but more so the hardships he endured, are telling on him. He is very weak now, but he is too proud to ask for anything, or even accept gifts when offered to him. Yet he is not too proud to eat and drink what they have left there, after they have gone."

Our curiosity was aroused, and we decided to avail ourselves of Mr. Rouleaix's kind offer to be our guide there on the following afternoon. We returned to the forest town on the train which brought back the labour force, and after enjoying a hearty supper, we witnessed a very good amateur performance in the theatre.

The following morning we strolled about in the pleasant town with its neat houses and pretty flower gardens, and in the woods, which in the immediate vicinity of the town were quite park-like. Coming back to the hotel, we rested awhile on the beautiful terrace, enjoying some refreshments, the little town and pretty valley spread before us like a panorama. How well everything is arranged for travellers in this happy and enlightened age! All they need is their credit card, the amount of what they get being punched off from it.

After dinner another train conveying labour force brought us to the foot of the peak. Mr. Rouleaix led us up on a winding footpath, past some very romantic scenery. Edith was somewhat fatigued when we reached the top.

Sure enough, there stood before us the poorest little log house imaginable.

At the sound of our voices a man emerged from it, with long white hair and beard, unkempt and shaggy, the skin of his face and hands looking like smoked parchment. The dress he wore was composed of rabbit skins, patched together with bark fibre. That miserable, savage-looking suit hung loosely on his shrunken limbs.

"What do you want up here?" he asked, in a croaking voice. "Why do you not stay down in your gilded slavery? Why will you pollute the air of liberty with your presence?"

Edith shuddered with disgust. "Let us go," she said. Nor could the disgust she felt be worse than that I experienced. It made me sick at heart comparing the two men, both woodmen, the one following the simple and easy rules civilisation imposed on all citizens alike—elegant, refined, accustomed to comfort and intellectual intercourse; the other boasting in the liberty of a maniac, a living caricature of man.

We turned to go down again. Mr. Rouleaix placed on the ground the basket with provisions that we had brought up, and followed us. I was shocked even more than Edith, and only gradually the lively conversation of Mr. Rouleaix dispersed the gloom this adventure had cast over me.

This evening we enjoyed some fine music, followed by a dance, in the theatre of the town.

After a hearty breakfast early on the following morning, we bid adieu to the pleasant valley and its jolly inhabitants, and the next train sped us further southwest.

CHAPTER V.

The great plains between the rivers Ohio and Mississippi, as well as those to the west of Mississippi and Missouri, are the prominent grain and fruit producers. A nephew of Dr. Leete, James Robson by name, was lieutenant of the Orchardist Guild in one of those western farming towns. Our train stopped at several of these towns, and it was a pretty sight, on one side of the depot the blocks of comfortable looking houses, with little gardens in the rear, grouped around the big square with the palatial public buildings, and on the other side the immense machine sheds, the electric works, the canning factory, the cheese and butter or condensed milk factories, the immense stables with surrounding pastures.

When we arrived at the farming town where Mr. Robson lived, we were met at the depot by that gentleman, a pleasant, jovial man of about thirty-five years, who conducted us to his comfortable home. His wife, a fine-looking woman, a couple of years the junior of her husband, her mother, a well-preserved matron, and two bright little cherubs awaited us there. Edith knew the family already, and they showed us so much ingenuous kindness that I, too, felt at home among them very soon. We did not stay in the public hotel of the town, accepting the offer of a nicely-furnished spare room in their house. Mr. Robson's working hours were in the morning, so he was at leisure to devote the rest of the afternoon and the evening to me. Mrs. Robson worked in the condensed milk factory, likewise in the morning, and, after we had partaken of a somewhat late dinner in the hotel, she took possession of Edith.

There was a big clock tower attached to the hotel, with a gallery running around it right under the spire. Under the guidance of Mr. Robson, I mounted the winding stairs, leading to the top, and came out on the gallery, where I had a most extensive view. The fields stretched as far as the eye could reach, being interspersed by orchards extending the full length of the fields. No fence was to be seen anywhere, excepting around the pasture at the stables. Mr. Robson explained to me, that at his grandfather's time they had laid out these mammoth farms, with not a shrub to relieve the eye. This not only had an evil effect on the people, creating melancholy, but it also fostered evil climatic influences. Since then the present system had been introduced. The fields are a mile in width, extending some fifteen or twenty miles, some even more, and in their whole length they were divided by strips of land planted with fruit trees. Rail tracks run out in every direction, so that the working force may lose no time in getting to the furthest ends of the farm land. Mr. Robson pointed out to me the kind and quality of the fruit trees in the various orchards, a great proportion of which were mulberry trees, an immense establishment for raising cocoons from silk worms belonging to the farm. He also informed me that corn, wheat, barley, oats and potatoes, constituted the main crops raised on this farm; to a smaller extent, but still on a grand scale, onions and vegetables were cultivated. Their rotation of crops was for a period of six years, after which the ground was for two years in grass and clover, thus returning humus to the land, which, besides, was kept rich by artificial fertiliser. The cattle manure was used for the vegetables. The farms in the south cultivated ramie to a great extent.

Afterward we passed through the flour mill and the canning establishments. They made no cheese and butter on this farm, except for their own consumption, condensed milk being the chief industry attached to their immense dairy. The stables were a marvel to me on account of their size as well as their commodious arrangements, the cattle being of the purest and most profitable breed. They were all fed indoors, the pastures being small and only intended for a few hours' exercise every day. Quite fatigued from our extensive walk and all the novelties I had seen, I returned as the night set in. After a hearty supper, which was sent for from the hotel, we had a pleasant chat together over our wine and cigars, the ladies not objecting to our smoking. Mr. Robson informed me that most of the wine was raised along the Pacific coast and on the hills between the Missouri, Arkansas and Mississippi rivers. Our conversation naturally drifted toward Mr. Forest's strange and incongruous assertions.

"I know something about it," said Mr. Robson. "I read it in the paper, and we had a good laugh about him. He says the farmers have but one general and one department chief, and are outvoted by the representatives of the other guilds.* The poor man's studies of the life in the nineteenth century must have been so intense that he mixes the past with the present, not knowing any more which is which. If by farmers he means all those who are

---

* Page 59, "Looking Further Forward."

occupied with the various labours done by farmers in the nineteenth century, then we have two departments, the Live Stock department, to which the fisheries are attached, and that of Soil Produce. The latter is a very great and important department, containing a number of guilds. There are the Foresters, the Orchardists, to whom I belong, the Cerealists, and so on. I read something about the farming life in the nineteenth century. I know they had small places; some of them so small that one man with his family had to do all the labour personally, having only a few primitive tools to do it with. Of course, there was toil from sunrise to sunset, to eke out a meagre subsistence, numbers of them living in poor one or two-roomed houses scattered in the woods or in the prairie—often miles away from the nearest neighbour—poor schooling for the children, no enjoyment. He must have thought we are living in that style yet."

"Surely!" I said. "He must think so. He mentioned that, though it would be impossible to build a theatre or concert hall at every country cross-road, still the number of such places in the city is out of proportion to those in country towns and villages, which has created a great deal of dissatisfaction."*

Mr. Robson laughed heartily at that. "Country cross-road is very good," he said, "and so is our dissatisfaction. What should we envy the city people for? Have we not libraries, theatre, and all other enjoyments as well as they? If we cannot have here the grand operas they have in the large cities, we can enjoy them occasionally in our vacations, and the invigorating influence of the free and open air is a boon that calls for envy rather than regret."

---

* Page 60, "Looking Further Forward."

"There's another thing to be taken into account, to use Mr. Forest's words," I said. "The nation is frequently left with small lots of goods on its hands, through changes of taste, unseasonable weather, and various other causes. These have to be disposed of at a sacrifice, and the loss charged up to the expenses of the business. It has been charged by the representatives of the farming population that such of these goods as are of poor quality are largely given out to farmers, while other things that are in first-class condition are disposed of in the storehouses of the cities at reduced prices, and that in such instances favouritism and corruption are coming in."*

Mr. Robson was highly amused at that. "Granted," he said, "that occasionally goods are left at the nation's hands, which have to be disposed of at a sacrifice. This is entirely correct. But what kind of goods are they? Mr. Forest says quite truly that these goods are less desirable through changes of taste and unseasonable weather. Now, where does the unseasonable weather come in? What kind of goods are affected by the weather? Can you imagine anything else but what we are raising on the farms? Of course, the greatest care is taken, but it cannot always be prevented to have some part of a crop slightly inferior by the inclemency of the weather. Now you may be sure that we keep only the best quality for our home consumption, being the best judges of their quality, and if some of the goods we send off are so markedly inferior that they have to be disposed of at a sacrifice, then it follows that only in the cities they will be used up. As for the other cause of less desirability, the change of taste, I plead guilty to the farmers suffering the loss

---

* Pages 60 and 61, "Looking Further Forward."

—if it is a loss, and not rather a gain. The taste does not change as quickly here as in the large cities, and we gladly avail ourselves of the chance of obtaining otherwise perfect articles manufactured in the cities, disposed of at a sacrifice, as it leaves a balance on our credit cards for procuring a variety of articles more desired by us. Now, where in the world could favouritism and corruption come in in such transactions?"

"That's settled," I exclaimed, more and more pleased to see Mr. Forest's gloomy Doubting Castle crumble to dust. "Another thing, however, he asserts: that the country people flock into the cities, and the nation would suffer from a want of agricultural products if all the people crowding into the large cities would be accepted. But they are not welcomed. They are appointed to farm work. That settles their desire to live in the cities, and at the same time destroys their ambition. The country people are satisfied that they cannot improve their lot, that they have to do farm work, and that the city people are imposing on them. The consequence is that they are working as little as possible, and the farming products have decreased to such an extent that city workmen of class B of the third grade have to be appointed to farm work, in order to protect the city people from starvation."[*]

Mr. Robson smiled. "Let me answer his last assertion first! We have in our library here some pictures of farm life in the nineteenth century. One of these pictures represents a forest. A miserable hovel, built up of raw logs, stands in midst of a small clearing, and two men are employed wielding big axes and chopping away at immense trees, while

---

[*] Pages 89 and 90, "Looking Further Forward."

a poorly-dressed woman is cooking at a fire out of doors, and a few half-clad children roll about in the grass. Another picture represents the same miserable hovel, with a low porch added and a rawish looking chimney at one end. The trees are a little further back. There is a field of apparently two acres' size, surrounded by an uncanny-looking zig-zag fence; a man ploughing in the field; one horse pulls the plough, and he is holding it, using all his strength. The other man and the woman, with bent back, are wielding mighty hoes, breaking the shining strips of sod, turned by the plough. If that was farm work in the nineteenth century, then I wouldn't wonder if they had preferred the city. And if our farm life would be such, as Mr. Forest seems to think, then I would not blame them for working as little as possible. But how different it is with us! We have our few hours of labour, and we go there, when our turn comes to relieve the set of men working before us. The machine does the work, always steady, always the same, neither more nor less. Once on the machine, we have to attend to it, willy-nilly. And as to the country people crowding into the cities, that is only one side of the question. There are just as many city people coming to work among us in the country. The fact that a person is born in one place does not compel him or her to live there always during a lifetime. When the young people have passed through their three years' apprenticeship, so that they may select their profession, they find here quite a variety to choose from—three or four guilds, not to speak of the different branches, being always represented in a farming town. But there are some persons who have a special liking, some special faculty or aptitude, for a particular trade, art or science, to study which to perfection and to practise which, a constant residence in the city is required. *The schools of technology, of medicine, of art, of music, of histrionics, and of higher liberal learning, are always open to aspirants without condition. Of course, some may honestly mistake their vocation, but finding themselves unequal to the requirements of the schools, drop out and return to the industrial service; no discredit attaches to such persons, for the public policy is to encourage all to develop suspected talents.** Thus, every year, some young men from farming towns move into the large cities for the purpose either to study or to enter a guild for which they have a special aptitude. On the other hand, there are numerous young men in the cities who would prefer country life, and who gladly avail themselves of an opportunity to do so, whenever it opens. In all our farming and forest towns a number of machinists are employed to keep our numerous machinery in constant good order, make minor repairs, and, when necessary, set up and adjust new ones. Only first class first grade men of the Machinist Guild are sent from the cities for these positions, and they are greatly coveted, as much independence and importance is attached to them. It is the great ambition of a young man bred in a farming or forest town, when he succeeds in entering the Machinist guild in the nearest city, to return in after years to his birthplace as machinist of the town."

Edith and Mrs. Robson by this time being ready to go out, and the children put to bed and under the guardianship of their grandmother, we took a stroll through the well-lighted street up to the great square. It was a fine night, very mild for the season, and many promenaders were met with in the park

---

* Page 72, "Looking Backward."

around the public buildings. We afterward entered the theatre. The first play was just over, and we enjoyed yet a very good comedy, very ably executed, and some very fine singing.

On the next day I had a delightful stroll with Edith in one of the many orchards. We all had dinner together at the hotel, and in the afternoon Mr. Robson took us out into the fields on a small electric car. We witnessed the ploughing and harrowing by electricity, and the electric drilling machine planting the wheat. Our electric car brought us about twenty miles off from the town, when a broad ditch impeded our further progress. Mr. Robson then told us that the fields across the ditch belonged to the next farming town, which was about eighteen miles distant. There was a bridge across the ditch on the main road. We passed along the ditch for a considerable distance, and then entered another track that brought us back to the town, running between an orchard and an immense clover field. Other machines were at work there. Some mowing the clover, others converting it into hay by a quick process, and others again loading a train of cars standing on the track ready to deliver the hay into the immense barns back of the depot.

The next morning we left for Boston on a different route, stopping a day in New York.

CHAPTER VI.

We had returned, and, the vacation being over, we resumed our daily occupations. I felt happy. Happy in the love of my sweet wife, in whom I discovered new charms every day; happy in the company of her refined and kindly disposed parents;

happy in the pursuit of my new avocation. I had brought with me from the country a freshness and vigorous delight in the existing conditions which lent more strength and power of conviction to my lectures.

I had one more discourse with Mr. Forest, explaining to him how mistaken he was concerning the farming population. The poor man, wrapped in his own notions, merely shook his head and gave me up, seeing that I was no longer a subject for him to experiment on. He never conversed on his gloomy notions with me any more after this, seeing that my credulity was gone. Yet some of his objections that appeared logical to me lingered in my mind yet, and I was longing for the promised discussion between him and Professor Yale.

Finally the appointed day came. The whole city was expectant; and to give a chance to every one who took an interest in witnessing the discussion, the Grand Opera House was chosen for the purpose. I was fortunate to get a front seat, with Edith to my right, and Dr. Leete to the left of me. The magnificent hall was brilliantly lighted, and every available place in it was filled. The beautiful curtain was down. Seats were placed for the two gentlemen on the stage in front of the curtain.

The bell rang. Mr. Forest and Mr. Yale appeared, bowed to the public, and the controversy commenced.

Mr. Forest was the first one to speak. Holding up a bundle of papers, containing his notes, he said:

"Ladies and gentlemen! It inspires me with hope for the future, that this evening to me is given a chance to open your eyes about the abyss, on the verge of which we all are wandering. I mean to demonstrate to you that our organisation of society, with its pretended basis of human equality has proved to be a failure—that there prevails to-day an inequality in many respects more oppressive than that of the nineteenth century—that favouritism and corruption are about as potent under our communistic rule as they were at the end of the nineteenth century—that personal liberty is almost entirely destroyed—that the members of the industrial army, without having the right to vote at the election of their superiors, are at the mercy of their officers—that the members of the industrial force, who are considered enemies of the government, are leading a life that may be very properly styled as twenty-four years of hell on earth—that since abolishment of competition the people are mentally degenerating for want of intellectual exercise, and that not even a greater wealth is a consolation for the loss of the greater liberty and independence the people enjoyed in the last century, as the shortening of both the years and the hours of productive labour, abolition of competition and the increase in the number of consumers have reduced the average daily income of the inhabitants of the United States to such an extent that the amount inscribed on our credit card is so small that it affords only a very frugal living to the people of the twentieth century."*

Mr. Forest paused, and Professor Yale, who had been making shorthand notes, now addressed him:

"Mr. Forest, I have noted down all your assertions, and now I propose that you take them up one by one, so that after you have given your arguments on one of your assertions, I may state what I have to say on the subject, and that we finish each single assertion, before you take up the next one."

"I agree with your proposal," said Mr. Forest.

---

* Pages 93 to 94, "Looking Further Forward."

"Then I have only one more request," added Professor Yale, turning to the audience, "that this assembly may elect an umpire to decide disputable points on the right of having the floor."

A low murmuring passed through the whole assembly of about forty thousand persons. Suddenly a voice cried: "The man of the nineteenth century!" Laughter and clapping of hands followed; then it rang through the whole building: "Mr. West!" "Mr. Julian West!" "Professor West!"

I rose, and when the storm had subsided, I bowed and acknowledged my thanks for the confidence expressed. I then asked permission of the two combating gentlemen to remain on my seat, which they granted.

"The first thing for you to prove, Mr. Forest," said Professor Yale, "is that our organisation of society with its basis of equality has proved a failure, and that there prevails to-day an inequality more oppressive than in the nineteenth century."

"Exactly," was Mr. Forest's answer. Then he turned to the public: "Ladies and gentlemen, look around! Is the leading principle in creation equality or inequality? You find sometimes similitude, but never conformity. Inequality is the law of nature, and the attempt to establish equality is therefore unnatural and absurd. We may just as well try to make every man six feet long, forty-two inches around his chest, with a Grecian nose, blue eyes, light hair and a lyric tenor voice, as to attempt to equalise all lives and reduce them to a communistic state. Consider, in connection with the difference in the mental and physical powers of men, their different inclinations and tastes, the variety of their occupations, and then say whether the establishment of society on the basis of communism, of absolute equality, is possible.* The question before us is a very plain one. Are we all alike? If we are not alike, if we differ in mental power and in physical ability, if the results of the labour of men are different, then there is no reason why the wealth of the nation should be equally divided.† Thus it is plainly seen that an organisation of society with a basis of equality is a failure. But more: We divide the workers into six classes for the reason that their ability differs. The inequality of men is thus distinctly recognised, but the products of labour are equally divided in the name of equality. Now, everybody has a natural right to the products of his activity, but we are taking a large share of the results of the labour of a clever worker of class A of the first grade, to give it to a lazy fellow of class B of the third grade. This is downright robbery.‡ We have, in the name of equality and justice, established the 'right' to rob an industrious man of a part of the product of his labour and give this booty to his lazy comrade.§ In the nineteenth century the labourers of the different trades had a perfect right to organise co-operative societies, and thus secure all the profit that was in their labour. If they would rather work for an employer, leaving the cares and risks of the management entirely to him, they had certainly no reason to complain of the profit of the employer.‖ And if they were not satisfied with their treatment, they could at any time seek other employment.¶ This shows that

---

* Pages 30 to 31, "Looking Further Forward."
† Page 31, "Looking Further Forward."
‡ Page 32, "Looking Further Forward."
§ Page 34, "Looking Further Forward."
‖ Page 33, "Looking Further Forward."
¶ Page 34, "Looking Further Forward."

to-day there prevails an inequality more oppressive than in the nineteenth century."

Mr. Forest bowed and sat down, and Professor Yale rose to address the vast audience:

"Ladies and Gentlemen: It almost seems to me an insult to this highly intelligent audience to refute the first part of Mr. Forest's arguments, their inconsistency being self-evident. Permit me, therefore, to pass them over with a few remarks merely. True, there is no equality in nature. Every plant differs more or less from the surrounding ones; but they all rest securely in their common soil. They all alike enjoy the genial rays of the sun, giving them light and warmth, the refreshing rain, aiding in their development. But, while they all share equally in these boons, there is inequality, variety in their size, their colours, their general appearance, their fruits. Thus with us. We all share alike the great boon we derive from our combined labour under our present system —the credit card. But as our tastes differ, we make different use of it, everyone according to his or her inclination; and it certainly does not trouble any well constituted mind that we are not equal in size, colour of the eyes, or the sound of the voice. To infer from the inequality of physical phenomena that there should be no equality in justice and in natural right, is both illogical and absurd. It would be like carrying owls to Athens to say any more on this subject.

"But Mr. Forest says that to-day there prevails an inequality more oppressive than in the nineteenth century. His objections are, and his arguments rest on the fact, that our credit cards are all alike, and that the clever worker of first class, first grade, receives the same recompense as the less experienced worker of class B, third grade, and he calls that downright robbery. He uses, in speaking of class B, third grade, the epithet 'lazy fellow.' I am extremely sorry that an otherwise highly polished and well-meaning gentleman like Mr. Forest should thus grossly and by wholesale insult an immense number of his fellow-beings, the sixth part of our working force. Laziness with our system, where most of our labour is attention to and direction of the machine— laziness in most cases is impracticable, even if the worker should be so inclined, which again is very improbable with our short working hours. But some have to be the last, some must belong to the lower grades, and these generally are the younger members, rising gradually into higher grades, as they attain more perfection in their trades. The idea is absurd that the highest grade workers should consider it robbery to see their less experienced comrades enjoying the same recompense. What enables them to live in ease and comfort and security with such short working hours as we have, if it is not the combination of all the workers? Let the high grade worker stand alone, and soon he would be reduced to want and suffering, barbarism and savagery, with all his skill and energy. But it is needless to dwell any longer on this subject; it is well understood by all of us, and it was so even by the workers of the nineteenth century. Looking over the files of newspapers in that period, we find that in all strikes, in all adjustments between employer and employed, the wages finally agreed on were for all alike, the most skilful receiving the same as the less experienced worker in the same trade; and the leaders, who generally were of the highest capacity among them, insisted on it. None of the workers at that period thought that unfair, or a downright robbery. What they complained of was the great difference in the income of the employer and of the real worker. Mr. Forest has a great deal to say about the census of

1880. I own that it gives us very interesting statistics, and I will point out a few figures shown by it. I find there that at that time the employees of manufactories numbered 2,019,035 males above sixteen years of age, 531,639 females above fifteen years and 181,921 children. These were employed in 253,852 establishments, which represented a capital of $2,790,272,606. The wages paid in one year were $947,953,795, the value of the material was $3,396,823,549 and the value of the products $5,369,579,191. Now, granting eight per cent interest on the capital—a procedure which but few of the ladies and gentlemen present may understand correctly, as we have nothing in our system to compare with the monetary system of the nineteenth century—then there yet remains a profit of $801,580,039. This secured to the employer in the average $3157.66 and to the worker $346.90 per year. Yet, considering that vast numbers of these 253,852 establishments were merely small shops, the employer working himself, either alone or with the assistance of one or two men or a few children, and consequently earning a great deal less than the average of employers, but more than the average of workers—considering that, the difference in the income of the worker and that of the employer assumes vastly greater proportion.

"The difference between the income of the employer and the worker is better illustrated, if we investigate some particular manufactures. There is the manufacture of gas and lamp fixtures. With thirty-five establishments and working force of 3,069, the average income of the worker was $478.75, and of the employer $26,417.77. Twenty-one galvanizing establishments employed 501 men and seventeen children with an average income of $22,999.71 for the employer, and $472.58 for the worker. Fifty wood pulp factories averaged an annual income for the

Looking Beyond. 59

employer of $14,989.14, and $367.88 for the worker. There were 1,990 manufactories of woollen goods, averaging an income of $13,184.45 for the employer, and only $298.67 for the worker. Four establishments for jute and jute goods averaged $18,677.25 per year to the employer, and but $270.43 for the worker. 872 slaughtering and meat-packing establishments, employing 26,113 men and 1,184 children, averaged a yearly income of $24,497.06 for the employer, and $384.97 for the worker. In the manufacture of wool hats the average income of the employer was $36,007.30, and of the worker $346.10. Four lamp and reflector manufactories in Chicago employed 345 males over sixteen years of age, twenty-five females over fifteen years of age, and fifty-five children; the employer's income sums up to $51,852, and the worker's to $374.70. Dyeing and finishing of textiles was done in 191 establishments, the working force employed amounted to 12,788 males over sixteen years, 2,038 females over fifteen years, and 1,872 children. With a capital of $26,223,981, the expense for wages, $6,474,364, and for material, $13,664,295, and with a return of $32,297,420 for products, allowing eight per cent interest on the capital, the income of the employer averaged $52,674.57, and that of the worker $387.73. Thus, too, we find that of the 6,435 men, 9,473 women and 2,895 children employed in the manufactories of worsted goods the average yearly income of the worker was $301.60, and of the employer $55,578.58. These are a few items to show the inequality in the income of the workers and the employers in the nineteenth century. I might continue for a long time yet; but these few examples are quite sufficient. Under such auspices to say that to-day prevails an inequality more oppressive than in the nineteenth century, is simply absurd.

"Again, Mr. Forest says that in the nineteenth century the labourers of the different trades could have organised co-operative societies, and thus secure all the profits themselves. That had been tried repeatedly and invariably failed. The few items I just have mentioned show the great advantage capital had over labour. Any co-operation of working men could be and was easily crushed by a combination of capitalists. It lay in the competitive system, that the greater capital swallowed up a number of smaller ones, and the few of equal strength and power remaining combined, which rendered them next to omnipotent.

Finally, I will but mention the concluding remarks of Mr. Forest, that in the nineteenth century those workers who were not satisfied with their treatment could at any time seek other employment. So they could; but what good would it do them? They found the same conditions wherever they went."

Professor Yale bowed, and amid the applause of the audience he took his seat.

Then Mr. Forest rose again. "The learner professor of statistics," he said, with somewhat of a sneer, "has given you some figures, and made statements, to answer which at the present I am not prepared."

"And never will be," whispered someone audibly among the audience.

"Therefore," resumed Mr. Forest, "I shall give you my very just reasons and proofs for the next statement, namely, that favouritism and corruption are ruling, personal liberty is nearly destroyed, the members of the industrial army are at the mercy of their officers, and, if their voting relatives are considered enemies of the government, are leading a life of hell on earth.

"Under our system all recruits or apprentices belong for the first three years of their service to the class of unskilled or common labourers, assignable to any work at the discretion of their superiors, after which period they are allowed to select a special avocation. Thus the young man is during these three years at the absolute mercy of his superiors. They may assign him to easy and clean work, or they may send him to dirty and unhealthy jobs.* Records are kept for ability and industry, and upon these records they are assigned their places among the full workmen as first, second and third grade workers. High grading gives them the preference in selecting the trade they wish to follow.† Regradings take place at fixed periods, and when a man loses his grade, he also risks having to exchange the sort of work he likes best to some other less to his taste. The lieutenants, captains or colonels, are appointed by the generals of the guild, who in turn are under the command of the ten chiefs of the ten great departments. These officers may give their young friends, who enter the industrial army as apprentices, easy jobs and good records, and enable them, on the strength of their records after their first three years' service, to enter the first class of the first grade of a trade, when they are immediately appointable to a lieutenantship and can run up to the higher honours in a few years.‡ On the other hand, relatives of outspoken opponents of the administration can be placed in the second class of third grade of their trade, and their records can be so kept that they can never hope to secure a high position. They have practically to live worse than slaves, and are sometimes treated like footballs. Of course, they can go to a judge; but the minor judges being merely men who have passed the forty-

---

* Page 38, "Looking Further Forward."
† Page 39, "Looking Further Forward."
‡ Page 40, "Looking Further Forward."

fifth year and are appointed for five years by the president, they are of course trustworthy friends of the administration and not expected to decide against the officers of the government in favour of the 'Kickers.'* Such ill-used member has to go back to his position, where he will only be treated worse by his superior. And as the workers have no suffrage and nothing to say about the choice of their superiors, they are twenty-four years absolutely at their mercy.† If they want to have a good time, they must influence their friends, who have votes, to stand by the administration. Thus Congress has no influence. ‡ Many of the men and women from forty-five years upward spend their time in Washington 'hustling around,' trying to gain favours for their friends and for such people as address themselves to the hustlers. Millions of people who desire better work or promotion and who have no influence at home, write to the hustlers at Washington to secure their services. To enable some of our administration leaders to receive guests and entertain them with delicacies and wine, an applicant for favours has to give a part or perhaps nearly all of his credit card.§ We have in Washington a great many young women who prefer flirtation, fine meals and a fast life to the regular employment in the industrial army. They hold clerical positions in the different departments which are sinecures, and some of the higher officials spend fifty times the amount of their credit cards with these women, as I have been told.' ||

---

 * Page 41, "Looking Further Forward."
 † Page 42, "Looking Further Forward."
 ‡ Page 43, "Looking Further Forward."
 § Page 54, "Looking Further Forward."
 || Pages 55 and 56, "Looking Further Forward."

Here a general commotion throughout the house could be noticed, and a few cries of "Shame," but Mr. Forest quite unconcernedly continued:
"A part of their income is obtained by those seeking favours, who willy-nilly give up a part of their credit cards. Another part of the values squandered by influential persons comes from the public storehouse, where only a small proportion of the values taken out is pricked from their credit cards by the clerks, who would otherwise risk to be degraded to class B of their third grade.* And to conclude: the number of positions at the command of the government is very large. There is one lieutenant or overseer to about twelve men or women, not to mention the captains, colonels, etc.; and the amount of bookkeeping done is simply enormous. We are keeping books in all the producing as well as in the distributing departments, and every citizen has an account in the police books. Our population is now estimated at 500,000,000, which figure I arrive at by increasing twenty per cent for every decade since 1890. The complicated system of bookkeeping and the shortness of working hours granted to the bookkeepers, who are favourites of the members of the administration, make it necessary to appoint a bookkeeper for every fifty people. This gives to the government a chance to provide at its own pleasure over 10,000,000 of men and women with clean and easy work. Add to these 10,000,000 of positions about 10,000,000 officers of the industrial army, add furthermore the clerkships in the distributing places and many other preferred positions, then we can see at a glance what an enormous power the administration possesses, and

---

* Page 56, "Looking Further Forward."

how tempting this power is."* Mr. Forest took his seat again, and Professor Yale rose.

"These are many accusations in one breath," he said, "and it is well that I made shorthand notes of all, so that I may not omit to refute one; for refute them I will, one and all. Regarding his first general accusations about the ill treatment of our workers by their superiors, it is clearly seen that Mr. Forest's veneration of the nineteenth century has taken possession of him so completely that he mixes the conditions of that period with the present. Let us suppose under the conditions of the nineteenth century some great work to be done, as cutting a canal through an isthmus, the digging of a tunnel through a chain of mountains, or a bridge across a strait which divides continents. Under the then prevailing system a company or association would be formed of shareholders, that is, of persons who contributed certain sums with the expectation of reaping an immense benefit. Their own self-interest would induce them to appoint for the superior manager of the works the most able civil engineer available, who in his turn would appoint for the different branches superintendents who well understood their business and were capable to execute his orders. But many of the foremen or overseers appointed by them would be a different class of people. They would be mostly men of little or no education, who by fawning or some other mean trait wormed themselves into the confidence of their superiors, and thus rose above their former fellow-workers. With such men naturally favouritism and corruption would rule. They would assign those men who bribed them or fawned on them to the easier jobs, and those that were averse to them to the

---

* Pages 45, 46 and 47, "Looking Further Forward."

dirier and more dangerous jobs. And the men themselves, generally recruited from a floating population of common labourers, mostly without education, kicked about in the world, ill-treated and ill-paid since childhood, knowing that they find the same conditions wherever they work, with no choice but either to accept such treatment during ten or twelve hours' work with liberty at least for the rest of the twenty-four hours, or to starve, or to have worse treatment in workhouses or penitentiaries—they had to submit.

"How different it is with us! Our young men enjoy their childhood and their youth. They have, all, without exception, the best possible education until twenty-one years of age, and then they are assigned to their work. The tasks are easy, the hours short, the recompense most ample, for all alike, the third grade worker the same as the president. We give more hours of labour to the preferred pursuits, less hours to those most objectionable. Dangerous jobs we have not in our common routine of labour. You all know that *whenever the unavoidable difficulties and dangers of a pursuit are so great that no inducement of compensating advantages would overcome men's repugnance to it, then the administration only needs to take it out of the common order of occupations by declaring it 'extra hazardous,' and those who pursue it especially worthy of the national gratitude, to be overrun with volunteers.* There are numerous young men present in this hall *who are greedy of honour and would not let slip such an opportunity. Of course, we have abolished anything like unhygienic conditions or special peril to life and limb. Health and safety are conditions common to all our industries.** And now let us consider the

---

* Page 68, "Looking Backward."

young men of one class! They all know one another perfectly since childhood. They learned their alphabet together and their multiplication table, and they rose together from year to year into the higher classes. Their education is finished when they are twenty-one years old, and then you may justly consider them a band of brothers. Now their toil begins; not a very severe one, not many hours in the day, but they have to use all their will power, all earnestness, to fulfil what is required of them; they have to accomplish a task. They are still together, for three years yet, under the same officers, that band of brothers who know everyone's ability and character since childhood, who see every day how their comrades fulfil their tasks; they see the records kept daily and are competent judges of the justice of such records. Now let us bear in mind that they are highly educated, have plenty of leisure, no want, no cares, that they possess all the ardour, elasticity and enthusiasm of youth, and let anyone, who can, imagine that they would permit one man, even if he is their superior, to falsify the records, to give bad records to deserving young men on personal grounds, or the best records to the most backward on account of relation or friendship! Why, all the youth of the nation would revolt from one end of the country to the other, before they would submit to that. The three years passed, their records decide to what grade they belong; no friendship, no relation can change this. Then the old alliance is broken up, they choose different trades, new acquaintances, new friendships are formed, but still the proud spirit of independence, created by education, leisure and competence remains and *cannot* be stamped out any more. Mr. Forest says, the workers are twenty-four years at the mercy of their superiors, because they have no suffrage and nothing to say about the choice of their superiors. Well, suffrage they have to a certain extent, as the voting for communal works and such like, but they have really nothing to say about the choice of their officers. What of that? The ex-members, the men who have passed through their twenty-four years' service as workers, certainly have the most experience, and are therefore the most able to elect the general of the guild they used to belong to, among the superintendents or colonels of their guild, and as they themselves are entirely independent, and provided for the rest of their lives, without any more labour being exacted from them, it is self-evident that they would not give their votes for general to any superintendent whom they or their fellow-workers had found unjust, when they had to work under him. So it is pretty certain that under our system only a highly able, well meaning and fair minded man will be elected general, and he certainly will remain so, if he has any ambition to be elected department chief after his five years' service. And such a man, with no inducement whatever for corruption, surely can be trusted to appoint all the officers under him, especially as the choice of candidates is limited—the lieutenants from among the first class first grade workers, the captains from among the lieutenants, and the colonels or superintendents from among the captains. However, it is well known to all of you that a movement is on foot to give each company of workers the right to elect their own minor officers, reserving only the superintendency to be appointed by the general, and it is most probable that the next Congress will give it a trial.

"Mr. Forest says, furthermore, that if one of the workers has a complaint against an officer, the judge, being appointed by the president for five years, and, therefore, a friend of the administration, will not decide against an officer of the government, and will send such worker back to his position, to be treated worse than before by that officer. Now, let us consider first, what interest would the president have to take up the part of the lieutenant or captain against the worker? He has not appointed them; they cannot benefit him in the least; so why would he try to induce a judge always to decide in favour of the officer, right or wrong? And even if he would, what would the judge care about it? When the judge accepted the appointment of the president, he conferred a favour on him and on the community; for his term of labour was passed; he could enjoy the rest of his life in tranquility. He accepted an extra charge, for which there was no obligation. Besides, in most cases, the president would be out of office before him. He had nothing to expect from the president, nothing from the accused officer. They could not benefit him, nor could they ever harm him. But there certainly is one thing the judge has to care about, that is public opinion. If ever there is a complaint against an officer—which, indeed, is very rare—then you may be sure there are plenty of witnesses; and could it be supposed that they would pass it by quietly if the judge would make an unjust decision? You all know that anyone can publish a book or pamphlet, if he gets sufficient subscribers to cover the expense, by having their portion of the expense punched off their credit cards. The same system prevails with our newspapers and other periodicals.* Therefore, we have the most positive means to have the voice of the people heard by the people. And, in such a case as Mr. Forest asserted, pamphlets and magazines and the newspapers would ring with it from one end of the country to the other. *The claim*

---

* Pages 166 and 167, "Looking Backward."

of the workmen to just and considerate treatment is backed by the whole power of the nation. No officer is so high that he dares display an overbearing manner toward a workman of the lowest class. Not only justice, but civility, is enforced by our judges.*

"Next, Mr. Forest says: Congress has no influence, because the voters have to stand by the administration, to secure a good time for their friends in the industrial army. That would indeed be a queer kind of favouritism! How can an administration show favours to the *majority* of a people? That is just as amusing as his assertion of the 'hustlers' in Washington. Imagine a number of men and women upward of forty-five years, instead of enjoying their years of rest in ease and comfort at home, or in travelling and seeing new sights, instead of that 'hustling around' to gain favours for millions of people who write to them. Why! I never knew that Mr. Forest could produce so much genuine humour. How many men are there in Washington who could give favours, if such a thing as giving favours would be in vogue with us? There's the president, there are ten department chiefs, and about one hundred and fifty generals, the few members of the board of regents and the inspectorate, not two hundred persons in all. Well, they have to eat and drink; they have to do something at least, some time during the day; they certainly could not make '*arrangements*' with more than five of these hustlers in a day. Now, supposing that each and every one of these less than two hundred highest functionaries would *arrange*' matters with five of these hustlers every day; that would give a chance to nearly one thousand hustlers in a day. He says they have to 'work

---

* Pages 206 to 207, "Looking Backward."

for millions of people. What is 'millions'? More than one million, two millions at least, rather more; but let us say two millions. Then every one of these thousand hustlers would have to get favours for two thousand persons in the year, that is about seven every working day; and with all the letters to write, that would keep them pretty busy, and the high officials in Washington, too. I cannot see what time would be left for their legitimate duties. And all this just for the fun of the thing? Oh, no! Mr. Forest tells you, that all these applicants for favour have to give up a part, or perhaps nearly all of their credit cards. Supposing they could do it, what would they live on then? Would it not be wiser to ask no favours and enjoy the good living their credit cards secure them without any favour? But they cannot do it. *Our credit cards are not transferable, but strictly personal.** *If we don't spend our allowance, it is permitted to accumulate to a certain extent, when a special outlay is anticipated. But unless notice to the contrary is given, it is presumed that the citizen who does not fully expend his credit, did not have occasion to do so, and the balance is turned into the general surplus.*† So it is plainly seen, that idea of giving up parts of the credit cards is merely one of the wild fancies of the very learned gentleman. But amusing and risible as these two last-named notions or accusations of Mr. Forest are, the one next in order is an outrage, I might almost call it a blasphemous calumny. To insinuate that a beautiful young lady, reared in ease and comfort, intellectually and morally trained to the highest attainable perfection up to the age of

---

* Page 88, "Looking Backward."
† Page 89, "Looking Backward."

twenty-one years, with light tasks and plenty of leisure, with a certainty of having all her wants, her comforts and desires supplied during her lifetime, with no barrier to part her from the man she loves—to insinuate that such a happy creature would prefer a life of shame, the very name of which, fortunately, is obsolete in our time—is the height of insult. He says he has been told so. No doubt he has, and our young men will pardon him on the plea of monomania; but it is a cruel and a detestable joke of him who practised it on the poor man's credulity."

An awful silence reigned all over the immense hall; not a breath seemed to stir among the forty thousand people assembled, and looking at Mr. Forest, I could not help pitying him, as he was leaning back in his chair, white as marble, and his forehead and eyes covered with his right hand.

Professor Yale continued: "The idea that the sample clerks would only punch out a small portion of the value taken out from the public storehouse by the higher officers, is preposterous. Such a thing could never happen with us, where the sample clerk pricks out the value and immediately sends the order by pneumatic process to the storehouse, where likewise a copy is retained, entering it at the same time in the account book, which is kept for everyone. And all these books are open to public inspection, and everything has to tally.

"Finally Mr. Forest speaks of the enormous power the administration has for finding easy places for its favourites, and illustrates it by a number of wild statements. First of all, he forgets that the president has nothing to do with the appointment of such officers, as every general appoints the officers under him, being himself elected. He says there is one lieutenant or foreman to about twelve men or women, which is absolutely false; the average being one to fifty, in some trades more, in some less. And if he adds the amount of book-keeping done is simply enormous, what does he mean? Does he know so little of the institutions he is living under that he thinks we have special book-keepers for all accounts? Does he not know that the officers have to keep the records, which are always open to public inspection? He calls them POLICE records, thinking of the nineteenth century. Does he not know that the sample clerks have to keep the accounts of the credit cards, that the distributing clerks keep their own accounts, and that only comparatively few clerks and book-keepers are permitted to the superintendents and generals to assist in regulating the produce? He says our population is estimated at 500,000,000. Where does he get these figures? According to the census of 1990 we are far off from half that number yet. But Mr. Forest has his own way of statistics, and he arrived at this figure by counting twenty per cent increase for every decade since 1890. Yet there only was a twenty per cent increase from 1890 to 1900; after this the percentage of increase sank gradually from decade to decade, until now it is less than ten per cent. And this is borne out by general observation; for we all know that, as nations grow older, the number of their inhabitants does not increase so rapidly as it did when these nations were in their infancies. Why, even in 1890, in Germany, among a nation remarkable for large families, the increase of the population had been found less than ten per cent in a decade. And it is a generally acknowledged fact, which was even known already in the last century, that in continued general prosperity

Looking Beyond. 73

people do not multiply as fast as they do in prosperous periods preceded by hard times. This is quite obvious to those who have studied anthropology and sociology. But to return to Mr. Forest's figures. He counts a book-keeper for every fifty people, thus bringing out at his own figures an army of 10,000,000 book-keepers, to whom he adds 10,000,000 officers of the industrial army, and if he is as lavish with the sample and distributing clerks, whom he only mentions, he might bring up his army of what he calls non-producing favourites, to about 30,000,000. That's the reverse of the medal, Mr. Forest's own figuring. Now let us look at the face of the medal, the actual figures! The 10,000,000 book-keepers he dreams about dwindle down at once to less than 50,000, two or three for each superintendent, and from ten to fifty to each of the generals, department chiefs, the president, and other high functionaries in Washington, together with those employed on statistics. The number varies according to the amount of work required. The lieutenants at the rate of one to fifty workers, the captains at an average of one to 500, and the superintendents at about one to 5,000 workers (in some guilds more, in some less), at that rate our officers, including the highest functionaries, number about 1,650,000, which is near the correct figure. The clerks in the sample stores average about one to 1,000 inhabitants, while in the distributing places they may be averaged at one to 5,000. All this added brings out a force of nearly 2,000,000, all in all, of what Mr. Forest calls preferred positions, and not 30,000,000, as according to his standard. But it must be borne in mind that the president has nothing to do with the appointment of these men. The generals, who themselves are elected, do this, each one in his particular guild. And then let me add that these positions are not preferred at all, as they impose on those so employed generally more hours of labour than some of the trades."

CHAPTER VII.

A tremendous applause followed, after Professor Yale had sat down, and it was some time before Mr. Forest so far composed himself as to rise and to address the public again:

"In comparing our time with the last century, we miss now the great power of competition they had then, which was permanently spurring everybody to use his best efforts to elevate himself and humanity.* Thus we are mentally degenerating for want of intellectual exercise. And in sight of all these deplorable retrogressions we cannot even console ourselves with possessing greater wealth. The decrease of production as well as the increase in the number of consumers have reduced our average daily income far beyond that of the nineteenth century.† According to the census of 1880 the whole industrial army of that day numbered 17,392,099 out of an entire population of 50,155,783; only 2,647,157 of this working force being girls and women, including the servant girls. Of the people under fifteen years of age 1,118,356 were employed, and out of the men and women over sixty years 933,644 were males, and 70,873 females.‡ Thus that census shows that over twelve per cent of the population of the United

---

* Page 114, "Looking Further Forward."
† Page 93, "Looking Further Forward."
‡ Page 86, "Looking Further Forward."

Looking Beyond. 75

States belonging to the industrial army were under fifteen and over sixty years of age, and there lived 15,527,215 persons of the age that would make them to-day members of our industrial army. They employed therefore, 2,173,184 more persons than the whole population between the ages of twenty-one to forty-five numbered. Therefore they furnished a stronger working force than does our generation.*

Now in that day the people engaged in the occupations, trades and professions that we would call non-productive numbered 1,654,319, including all the servants. Deducting these from the 2,173,084, under the age of fifteen and over sixty, there still would be a surplus of 518,765 women and men of that time over the number of people that would belong in our days to the industrial force. So they had undoubtedly in 1880 a surplus of productive persons above the age that would place them in our industrial army, which amounted to over three per cent of persons of the age where they to-day would have to be members of the industrial army.† Deduct all ladies occupied by their duties as mothers, before and after the birth of their children, deduct all persons permanently sick, cripples, and others unable to do productive work, and consider that these people in the nineteenth century were stimulated by competition, and you must admit that they could obtain more and better work than we can to-day. They also worked longer hours than we do,‡ and we squander a greater amount of labour in overseeing and book-keeping.§ Thus the productive power is lessened, and therefore the production decreased. As our people live

---

* Pages 86 to 87, "Looking Further Forward."
† Page 88, "Looking Further Forward."
‡ Pages 88 to 89, "Looking Further Forward."
§ Page 90, "Looking Further Forward."

longer than they did in the nineteenth century, taking life easy, the number of consumers is larger in proportion than at that time.* Hence it follows that the average income is smaller to-day than it was one hundred years ago."

Professor Yale took the stand again. "Mr. Forest sorely misses the great power of competition, which, as he says, spurred everybody in the former century to use his best efforts for elevating himself and humanity. Therefore, he says, we are degenerating for the want of intellectual exercise. This is one of his very amusing statements, and little is needed to refute it. COMPETITION, which brings out the worst passions in man, which PUNISHES men for the finer qualities, as GENEROSITY, TRUTHFULNESS, INDEPENDENCE, MAGNANIMITY, and which ranks him highest who has the least regard for his fellow-men—that *curse of former ages*—thank God! we know no more of it. But Mr. Forest says it spurred everybody to use his best efforts to *elevate himself and humanity*. That is rich indeed, and so is his statement that we degenerate for want of intellectual exercise. Intellectual training, systematically practised in our schools until the age of twenty-one, that is no intellectual exercise, oh no! And during the twenty-four years of labour that follow, as well as the remainder of his life, there is no occasion for intellectual exercise, when everyone has leisure, has libraries, museums, art galleries, debating clubs and —what not?—at his disposal! Oh, no! With numerous distinctions of honour to spur his ambition to great efforts—there is no intellectual exercise, oh, no! It seems, Mr. Forest recognises intellectual exercise to consist of mere struggle for exist-

---

* Page 92, "Looking Further Forward."

ence, in which the competitor seeks to acquire, without equivalent return, the product of the labour of others, and then certainly the now almost extinct wolf would be the most intellectual being. The system of the nineteenth century COMPELLED competitors to be beasts of prey, seeking whom they might devour, and so darkly obscured the intellect of their victims, that they called a man smart "who dishonestly acquired great ill-gotten wealth. Shall we return to that system?"

As from one stentorian throat came a thundering "No," which shook the building.

After the storm of indignation had subsided, Professor Yale continued: "But Mr. Forest again tried his hand at some figures, and, starting with the census of 1880, he attempts to prove that they had a stronger working force at that time than we have. Now, I mean to show you that just the reverse is the case, in spite of the criminal recklessness of that age, which made them employ children and old men and women at hard labour. The figures Mr. Forest takes from the census of 1880 are correct enough, but he certainly does not apply them correctly. As he seems blind to the evidence of social comforts in the everyday life around him, and to prefer dry calculations based on that census, I shall also adopt it in my refutation of his erroneous deductions.

"He states, correctly, that there had been in 1880 a population of 50,155,783 in the United States. All men, women and children employed or active in any trade or calling were 17,392,099. Of these we have to deduct all non-productive workers, and those whose functions are not required now. There are 25,467 clerks and copyists, 1,075,655 domestic servants, 64,137 lawyers, 26,761 men in the army and navy, 115,531 officials and employés in government, state, county, city, or town service, 13,384 private watchmen and detectives, 77,920 persons employed in personal service not specified, 18,523 agents, 445,513 clerks and salesmen in stores, 481,450 traders and dealers, 81,649 commercial travellers, peddlers, etc., 30,928 persons employed in banking, 17,750 in insurance. Deduct furthermore 64,698 clergymen, whose services with us are private, 68,461 employed in saloons and bar-rooms, and 77,740 of various non-classed orders engaged in private transportation. This sums up the non-productive or now obsolete trades and professions to 2,685,558.

"We see by the fifth annual report of the United States Labour Secretary, 1888-9, that the railroad companies employed 187 workers to every 100 they actually needed, so they always had an actual reserve force, counted but not worked and not paid, of 46.53 per cent. This system prevailed also in other branches; but as their statistics for the moment are not available, let them pass! So we deduct from the 250,453 railroad employés 46.53 per cent, or 116,535 workers. Thus we reduce the labour force of 1880, including children and old people, to 14,590,006 workers.

"And, again, our system of consolidating the labour of persons similarly employed renders superfluous a vast number of workers necessary under the former system, when they were scattered and antagonistic to each other. Thus *half* of the 133,856 persons employed in hotels and restaurants would have done more in half the time under our system; *one-fourth* of the 121,942 launderers and laundresses would have sufficed with shorter hours if they had been employed in large public laundries, such as are in use now; *half* of the 177,586 hackmen, draymen and teamsters, with only half their working hours, would have been more than needed. The same is to be said of the 44,851 barbers, the 85,671 physicians and surgeons, the 100,902 sailors, steamboatmen, pilots and canalmen; likewise the 131,426 fishermen, the 12,314 dentists and the 19,085 employed in boarding and lodging. This again gives a reduction of 383,330. We will not change the number of ostlers and servants in livery stables, nor of employés of the telegraph, street railroad and express companies, for although our centralised system involves a great saving of labour, yet the shortness of hours may be counted as offset.

"Again, there were in 1880 seven million, six hundred and seventy thousand, four hundred and ninety-three persons employed in agriculture in the United States. There were 4,008,907 farms, containing 536,081,835 acres, of which, however, only 284,771,042 were improved. This shows one person employed in one capacity or other on 37.125 acres. Yet it should be borne in mind that many of these farms were small, and the labour of a whole family often was confined to a few acres, which would still further reduce the acreage worked by one man. As our farms average from one to two millions of acres, and as we count one person for five hundred acres, even with our reduced hours, we need the labour of one man, where over thirteen had to be employed in 1880. But we will give Mr. Forest the benefit of doubt, as we can afford to be liberal, and will only mark one of our force to do the agricultural labour of eight in 1880, and deduct seven-eighths of their agricultural labour force, leaving 958,812. Even Mr. Forest's study of the nineteenth century must corroborate this statement, as there were even at that time some mammoth farms in the West and South, where, with the defective steam power, a few persons cultivated a large acreage with enormous increase of production. And, yet, what were they compared with ours? Now, there will remain as an equivalent to our workers the number of 7,495,000 or 14.95 per cent of the entire population, not forgetting that among them were children and old men and women.

"Now let us arrange that census according to our system! There were in 1880 among the population of 50,155,783, men and women from the age of twenty-one to forty-five to the number of 16,887,017, and not 15,527,215, as Mr. Forest would have it. *In his addition he falls short of over a million and a quarter.* We have on an average one lieutenant for fifty workers, one captain to ten lieutenants, and one superintendent to ten captains. We likewise have one sample clerk to one thousand inhabitants, one distribution clerk to five thousand; then the book-keepers and the higher functionaries, who all in all, according to the population of 1880, would amount to about 448,000. Add to these one to each ten thousand, employed on statistics and various minor duties, then you may figure up the non-productive workers to about 500,000 at the most. Deduct them from our working force, then you will have left yet 16,387,000 productive workers of the industrial army, or a percentage of 32.67 on the whole population.

"Thus, comparing the two systems, we find that the army of producers of 1880 is to that of the present day in the ratio of 14.95 per cent to 32.67 per cent, and this while granting that women, children and the aged produced as much as the flower of the nation, our present industrial army.

"But Mr. Forest says there is another drawback against us in the twentieth century, and he mentions all ladies occupied by their duties as mothers, before and after the birth of their children, all persons permanently sick, cripples and others unable to do productive work. That is true. But they had in the nineteenth century a vast number of workers marked as such in the census, but out of work part of the

Looking Beyond. 81

year. These were all the workers on a strike, or those temporarily out of employment by a lock-out, bankruptcies, by destruction of manufacturing establishments in consequence of fire, inundation or cyclone. Bricklayers and masons, carpenters, slaters, painters were out of work a considerable portion of the year; so were milliners, dressmakers, tailors, or any other persons employed for fabrics of fashion, which counted two busy and two slack seasons in the year. Let us be liberal, as we can afford it, and mark all these down as offset for the mothers nursing their babies, as well as for the permanently sick, the lame, the blind, the insane, who fortunately with us are very few.

"Again, note that there were $77,763,473 expended for fencing in one year of the former century, an expense which we have reduced to less than the thousandth part in proportion, no fencing being done, except around the small pastures, which are only used for the exercise of the stock—an immense saving, which enables us to spend more on magnificent public structures. Note, furthermore, that among the 2,732,595 men, women and children employed in 1880 in 253,852 manufacturing establishments, a vast proportion was working in small shops, with one, two or three persons to do the labour. They averaged 10.768 persons to one establishment; but as there were some employing one thousand and more persons, it follows that numerous establishments employed less than ten. We see there, for instance, that 28,101 blacksmithing establishments, employing 33,992 males over sixteen, eighteen females over fifteen years of age, and 516 children, averaged not quite $1\frac{1}{4}$ persons to the establishment; 10,701 wheelwrighting establishments, with 15,821 men, seventeen women and 270 children, average to a little over $1\frac{1}{2}$ worker to the establishment. Thus also plumbers and gasfitters, painters and paperhangers average $4\frac{1}{2}$; the 24,338 flour and grist mills average less than $2\frac{1}{2}$; saddlery and harness-making, a little over $2\frac{1}{2}$; tinware, copperware and sheet ironware manufacturing averages less than $3\frac{1}{2}$, and the cheese and butter-making two workers to the establishment. I could continue for a number of trades, but let these suffice! You can imagine the waste of labour with one or two persons working independently with their primitive tools.

"Again there are named among the industrial army of 1880 as many as 1,859,223 common labourers, a special class, not mentioned by me before. If you consider that they had nothing to work with but strong hands, and, may be, a pickaxe, shovel, or other primitive tool, while our common labour is done mostly with machinery to-day, and add that loss of labour to the loss of labour suffered by the small establishments as mentioned before, then you may commence to get an idea of the vast superiority of our system, and that we can afford to live longer, being able to get more than ten times the amount of products with less than half the hours of labour, employing none but the cream of the nation, the vigorous people from twenty-one to forty-five years. I do not think it necessary to add anything. We all know, of course, the great amount of necessities and comforts our credit cards guarantee us; but as Mr. Forest does not acknowledge facts, I had to follow him on his own ground step by step, arguing, drawing logical conclusions from the statistics he alone acknowledges, the census of 1880, and I sincerely hope I have succeeded."

The immense building shook with the applause that followed. Poor Mr. Forest took up his hat and passed out quietly. Some of the most intimate friends of Professor Yale, to whom Dr. Leete belonged, went up on the stage to shake hands with him, and they all were confident, that he could not miss the votes for getting the blue ribbon, perhaps the red one.

For my part I shook Professor Yale's hands with a sincerity coming from the bottom of my heart. Any faint doubts that had lingered yet were extirpated by the iron clad arguments of the clever professor of statistics.

CHAPTER VIII.

Next morning at breakfast the result of the discussion between Mr. Forest and Professor Yale was the topic of our conversation. The newspapers of the city were full of it, and the telegraph had carried the report of the shorthand notes to the most remote parts of the United States, as well as to the foreign countries enjoying the same blessings of our modern civilisation.

I had been delighted on the previous evening at having the last doubts removed that had been conjured up in my mind by Mr. Forest's arguments. This feeling prevailed with me yet; still I felt somewhat abashed at finding that I knew so little of my own time, and yet was employed as professor of the nineteenth century's history. This feeling took possession of me to such an extent that I gave it utterance while we were at breakfast.

"This need not trouble you at all," said Dr. Leete, in his kind manner. "Among your former contemporaries, there were comparatively few who understood what you used to call the labour question; and, as the nation was divided into classes, you, belonging to the privileged one, had no inclination to understand the wants and desires of the labouring classes, consequently took no interest in studying the statistics so important to them. All that which came under your own observation, is of sufficient interest to qualify you for lecturing on the nineteenth century."

This kindness on the part of Dr. Leete, the smiling approval of Mrs. Leete, and Edith's tender caresses reassured me, and with renewed vigour I entered into my task of lecturing.

The great excitement caused by Professor Yale's victory had also spread over the college. The learned gentleman's desk was richly decked with flowers, and thundering cheers from the lips of his students signalled his arrival. The same excitement had taken hold of my hearers, who greeted me with unusual warmth. Poor Mr. Forest looked rather downhearted. To the honour of the young men of the twentieth century I must say that they were exceedingly polite to Mr. Forest, while according to the practice of the nineteenth century they might have been supposed to gloat over his defeat.

A few hours later, during recess, I was enjoying my cigar in company and in conversation with the other professors of the college, when suddenly the door burst open, and a man about thirty years of age rushed in and ran up to Mr. Bowen, the professor of astronomy. He was his head assistant, who took his place in the observatory during his absence. Astronomy, like all the other sciences, has developed greatly during the last century, and every city of any importance has an observatory. The lenses, as I have been told and found out myself afterward, are more powerful than they were in the nineteenth century. The young man whispered a few words to Professor Bowen, who, on hearing them, immediately jumped up in the utmost excitement. He grabbed

Looking Beyond.

his hat and cane, and exclaimed, "Gentlemen, excuse me! A matter of the greatest importance."
He rushed through the door and among his own students. "No more lecture to-day gentlemen!" he shouted, "I am called off on a most important matter. You may go home." He rushed off again, and soon was out of sight.
We greatly wondered at this extraordinary behaviour, but, recess being over, we resumed our duties.
I had just closed my lecture when Professor Bowen came back. He beckoned me and the other professors, who were then leaving their respective rooms, aside, and said: "Gentlemen, come along with me. I will show you something that will make you rejoice to have lived to see it. To-morrow morning the journals will bring the news of it to every breakfast table on this continent, in Australia and in Europe, adding considerable parts of Asia and Africa. Come along! You will be grateful for having been among the first to see it."
We caught his excitement, we wanted to know more about it, but he only said: "Come and see!"
In a few minutes the electric car brought us to the observatory; we mounted the tower together. Expectantly we stood around the enormous telescope. He pushed Professor Yale forward and said: "Look! It is the planet *Mars* that you see."
Professor Yale did not look a long time before he uttered an exclamation of surprise, and when he left the telescope he was as excited as Mr. Bowen
My turn came next. It took me some time before my eye was adjusted to see the object before it.
"You must bear in mind that it is night on that hemisphere of Mars on which you are gazing," said Mr. Bowen.
Presently I saw a triangle, a right-angled triangle, very small apparently, but quite distinct and clear,

and as exact as mathematical instruments can make it. I gazed and gazed. Very indistinctly I could make out some lines in different directions, but bright and clear shone that wonderful triangle.

The other gentlemen took their turn each at the telescope, and then we looked at one another in mute surprise.

"What is the meaning of this?" finally asked Mr. Yale.

"What is the meaning of this?" repeated Mr. Bowen. "No more and no less than that the inhabitants of Mars wish to communicate with the inhabitants of the earth."

We fairly gasped with surprise; but there was no other explanation.

"That triangle is on the plain which we denote on our maps of Mars as *Prairie No. 3*," explained the professor of astronomy. Its hypotenuse cannot be less than three hundred miles long. This brilliant light in midst of darkness, these clear lines of mathematical precision can possibly be naught but the contrivance of intellectual beings. The civilised world will be in a flurry to-morrow and for some time to come. Something must be done to show our friends on Mars that we understand them, that our planet is peopled by beings of intellect as well as theirs. Come forward, Mr. Ward!" he added, addressing the assistant who had called him away from the college, and who modestly stood behind. "Come forward, sir! Let me shake hands with you! You were the one who discovered the triangle. To-morrow your name will be pronounced by every person as far as our modern civilisation reaches."

We all shook hands with the gentleman, who was quite overcome with emotion.

Great was the surprise of Edith and her parents when I brought home this wonderful news.

We read it over again the next morning, on perusing the journals after breakfast. Special meetings were held by the voters of every ward on that day, and resolutions passed, and telegrams sent off to Washington. The same happened in every city in the land, and, in most of the agricultural, forest and mining towns. Great excitement prevailed, and the wires were kept busy all day, the people clamouring for devising means to correspond with the inhabitants of Mars. That same evening our representative at the International Council, which this year meets at Constantinople, received instructions from Washington to that effect. Nor was the excitement any less in the other civilised countries. All the numerous observatories were beleaguered by crowds of persons eager to see the wonderful triangle. The phenomenon continued on Mars. Every time the night set in on that planet, the geometrical figure was seen.

The International Council in Constantinople was busy day and night. Our representative reported as follows:

"We decided that on some large plain a RIGHT-ANGLED-TRIANGLE should be formed by electric lights, having a hypotenuse of about 150 miles length, with the addition of the SQUARES DESCRIBED ON ITS TWO SIDES. I proposed to have it on the great plains of the West; but on the representation of astronomers, that a great plain where the atmosphere was nearly always free from clouds was necessary for the observation of such a large triangle, *the Libyan Desert*, part of which is reclaimed by artesian wells, was chosen by the Council to be the place on which our knowledge of geometry should be demonstrated to the residents of our neighbour planet. The enormous electric power required should be produced by utilising the cataracts of the Nile. The shortness of time in which this stupendous undertaking has to be accomplished, the great amount of machinery and immense number of labourers required, necessitate the co-operation of all civilised nations in this truly international work. Volunteers shall be called for in every country, and the work commence at once. Ferdinand Lorello, the most renowned civil engineer of the age, shall be appointed to direct the whole. He can make his plans and theoretical preparations while crossing the Atlantic, which may be accomplished in about four days. Lightning cars may bring him in a few days across Europe to Athens, where the lightning floating palace, "Aquila," may convey him to Alexandria and up the Nile. He shall appoint his own assistants, and give his orders by telegraph while travelling. At the same time the machinery, implements, tents, provisions and the labour force should be on the move from every country. The people of the various nations are requested to vote on the acceptance or rejection of these propositions at once, the whole labour force from twenty-one years upward being eligible to vote, as such immense withdrawal of workers from their regular occupations may necessitate an additional hour of labour for some time to come. An international badge of honour shall be given to every volunteer on his return."

This we read at breakfast on the fourth day after that wonderful discovery. It was followed by the publication of the order from Washington, that all labour not absolutely necessary should be dispensed with this day, and the vote of the people taken. Thanks to the perfect telegraphic system, there was not a family in the United States that did not read the same in the morning.

By noon the question was thoroughly discussed, and the voting commenced. The members of the various guilds assembled in their respective club

Looking Beyond. 89

houses, where the rear part of the stages served for improvised polling places, while in the front the counting of the votes was carried on as soon as one of the suffrage-boxes was full. An electric indicator, an invention for some time in vogue counted the votes as quick as six men could read them off. The audience hall was crowded with the members and honorary members of the guild, who returned to it as soon as they had voted. Great enthusiasm and rejoicing ruled everywhere, as vote after vote was reported containing the stereotyped " Aye." There was not one dissenting vote in any one of these polling places.

In the meantime the head statistician with a number of assistants was busy on the stage of the Grand Opera House receiving and booking the receipts as they came in. Gradually the house filled up by those who had done their voting and wished to witness the final result.

The clock struck six, when the last report had come in and was read aloud and booked. Soon afterwards the result (which was telegraphed to Washington immediately) was announced from the stage. Boston gave 631,523 "ayes" and not one "nay."

Tremendous was the applause that followed this announcement. Friends shook hands, others embraced, some wept with joy.

By this time the two hundred musicians of the grand orchestra had taken their usual seats, and the sonorous and stirring sounds of the anthem, "The March of Human Genius," filled the immense hall.

There was not much sleep that night. People went in and out the club houses, visited friends, listened to the reports made from time to time about the telegrams, as they came in.

Early next morning we read all the particulars

and discussed them at breakfast. The result had been the same everywhere as in Boston, unanimously assenting.

The same result was also cabled from Europe and other quarters.

The lightning ship "Arrow" had been waiting in port the previous evening with Mr. Lorello and his assistants on board, and as soon as the result was telegraphed from Washington, they started off across the Atlantic.

A number of ships was to leave during the day with the advance guard of volunteers, with machinery, provisions, tents and so on. Numerous men and machines were already busy loading at the ships, and the proclamation of the president, calling on volunteers, was published in every paper.

The president, in his proclamation, reminded those who would volunteer of the difficulties and hardships, and, possibly, sufferings they might endure. He reminded them that unaccustomed labour and a tropical climate awaited them; that sickness and even greater dangers might be in store for them, and that possibly many of them who ventured forth would return with shattered health, some perhaps not at all. For all this the only recompense would be the nation's thanks and the International Badge of Honour.

We were yet discussing these momentous events after breakfast, when the sound of the gong announced a visitor. Edith left the room and soon returned, ushering in Mr. Fest and Ellen Moore. Ellen was leaning on Mr. Fest's arm. Their faces were bright and beaming with joy and enthusiasm. They had just left the judge of our ward, by whom they had been married. They both had volunteered, and considered themselves extremely fortunate to be accepted. The rush of offers for volunteering had been

Looking Beyond. 91

so great, so far above the number requested, that lots had to be drawn to decide who should be the favoured ones to brave the danger and hardship, and to share in the nation's thanks. Ellen's brother likewise had volunteered, with numerous others of his age, but as they required two years of schooling yet, they were not accepted. Ellen had offered her services for the steam laundry in the main camp of the Americans, or as sick nurse in the hospital, or for any other service of the female auxiliary corps. Fest had volunteered to work in any branch of machine work or engineering, or, if necessary, as common labourer.

They were happy. Fest had succeeded to find solace for his wounded heart in the love of the sister.

What a strange courtship, and what an extraordinary honeymoon!

Edith was delighted, and their enthusiasm so much infected me that I likewise wished to volunteer, and it needed the clinging arms of Edith, the cool reasoning of Dr. Leete, and the energetic dissuasions of all to make me yield.

The happy couple took their leave, as their time was very limited, having to embark that very day.

Shortly afterwards we parted again, Edith to resume her duties in the ramie mill, I to lecture on the nineteenth century.

I could not let this opportunity pass without dwelling on the wonderful events to some extent. I told my hearers that there were some events in the nineteenth, as well as in preceding centuries, which caused universal excitement, enthusiasm and self-sacrifice, the same as we were witnessing and feeling ourselves at present. But what was then the object of such enthusiasm? It was *war*, popular war. Sometimes a grand idea had taken possession of a whole nation, or even nations. With the same fervour they rushed to sacrifice life and all they held dearest on the altar of their mother country, or for certain liberties, or for the realisation of some doctrines that had taken hold of the people. Sometimes it merely was national prejudice. But whatever the object may have been, the outcome invariably was the same, WAR, cruel, destructive war. Lacerated bodies, tens of thousands, and even hundreds of thousands of men, the flower of the land, in their premature graves, twice and thrice that number cripples for life! Weeping mothers, widows and orphans! Cities and villages consumed by flames; the harvest of the fields destroyed; ruin, desolation and misery! How different with us! The object is knowledge, the means are *labour*, dignified labour; labour that is ennobled almost to sublimity by the grand and lofty object, "KNOWLEDGE!"

In the course of a few days the fever heat of excitement had abated; but the strong yet placid undercurrent of enthusiasm remained. The daily labours were undergone as usual, but eagerly the contents of the papers were devoured every morning. Step by step we followed the doings of that devoted body from almost every part of the globe.

CHAPTER IX.

About six weeks had passed, when we received a letter from Mr. Fest, which was highly interesting.

"We live here as in a dream," he wrote. "Not that we can indulge in any dreaminess during our labours; hands and mind have to be pretty active and wide-awake. Our tasks are severe, the climate is enervating; yet if our labours would be twice as hard, none of us would complain. But the peculiar sensation that fills everyone out here is difficult to

describe. The strange surroundings, the wildness of
nature, the glaring lights with deepest shadows, the
phantasmagorial shifting of scenes, as I pass from
camp to camp, the babel of languages—all these
combine to make me feel doubtful of my own identity.
I have a sensation sometimes, as if behind the
physical eyes with which I see all objects around me,
there were another pair of incorporeal eyes, which
have the power to penetrate to the core of all I see.
Thinking over some events of history that always
seemed incomprehensible to me, I now have a sensation
as if I were living through them myself. I am
engineering one of the trains that pass over the improvised
rails from camp to camp, which is not without
danger, and requires the utmost of nerve and
skill I am capable of. You, in comfortable matter-of-fact
Boston, will undoubtedly find it strange that
during these trips I cannot get the crusades out of
my mind. As then the various nations of Christendom,
united for one purpose, under the same cloudless
sky, wondering alike at the strangeness of all
their surroundings, were yet divided in their separate
camps, speaking different languages—thus here, the
various nations of civilisation with their difference of
languages, of temperament and habits, in their different
camps, waved over by different flags, yet are
united for one purpose—LABOUR. Labour to break
another link in the chain of the arch-fiend of humanity,
ignorance! Labour, combined labour for
knowledge. It is grand. It seems to me the most
solemn prayer.

"Poor Ellen sees very little of her surroundings.
We have a large tent-hospital in our American tent-city,
which unfortunately is pretty well supplied
with invalids. You should see how devoted she is
to her duties as nurse, and how bravely she keeps it
up. Her praise is in everybody's mouth, and the

grateful convalescents spread the fame of *Sweet Ellen* beyond the limits of the American camp. It would do you good, also, to see the eagerness with which the convalescents long for the time when the physician will pronounce them fit for duty again.

"Everything is in good running order now; all our railroads are complete. The machines needed are all here by this time, and the ships are busy bringing up wire from the States, as well as from England, Germany and Sweden. France and Spain send the lamps, Italy the burners, and Greece the isolators. Most of our provisions come from Russia; some, too, from the Nile valley. The ships come up the Nile as far as Assuan. From there we have rails along the river as far up as the fifth cataract. At the bend above Dongola a railroad is constructed across the land to Khartoum, where we receive the posts, which come down the Nile from the Soudan. Branch roads lead likewise from the second and from the third cataract into the so-called desert. The second, third, fourth and fifth cataracts are to be utilised, and the work never ceases there. The German camp and that of the Scandinavians, both are near the second cataract; the American camp is a little above the third; the French and the Russian camps are between the fourth and fifth cataracts. The English camp is at Khartoum. The other camps are scattered over the desert. Numerous trains bring their necessities on the branch railroads; for their water supply many hundreds of artesian wells have been driven. In some unreclaimed parts of the desert, huge machines are at work, levelling the dunes. Long trains, carrying posts and wire, are continually on the road to the desert. There, machines, *manned by an engineer and a surveyor*, drive the holes for the posts, which are carried there from the vans on the back of camels. Men follow them to plant the posts, and to fasten the cross pieces and isolators. The posts are short—a little over man's height above ground. A machine follows them, rolling off and stretching the wire, which is fastened on the isolators by men standing on wagons. Behind them, other vehicles bring out the lamps, etc., and men on top of these wagons fasten these fixtures to the posts and connect them with the wires. Thus the work goes on continually.

"The hypotenuse of the triangle will be one hundred and fifty miles long. The lights along the lines of the whole geometrical figure, triangle as well as squares, will be five miles in width; the lamps one hundred feet distant from each other.

"While the work goes on briskly in the desert, the men of the river camps are busy leading off the water above the cataracts, constructing the buildings and putting up the machinery for the electric force works, setting posts and putting up the wires for the connection with the works in the desert.

"All these various, vivid pictures pass before me like the figures of a magic lantern, as I guide my train from camp to camp."

Shortly afterward we read that many thousands of blue spectacles had been called for, the eyes of many of the workers in the desert being badly affected. And so the days passed on, and we read every morning how the work progressed.

One morning the papers published a telegram, stating that the International Council had adjourned in Constantinople, to meet again on the banks of the Nile.

Nearer and nearer the day approached on which the works were to be completed, and then, finally, we read the report of our delegate at the International Council relating the grand success.

"When everything was ready," stated that report,

"Mr. Lorello ordered every living being off from the plains. He had invited us to witness the great event from an eminence at a safe distance from the hypotenuse, which place was connected by a wire with the electric works at the cataracts. It was a moonless night, and we had a very clear sky. Many thousands of the workers had assembled, in fact, every one whom not duty or sickness had kept away. We all wore blue spectacles, Mr. Lorello having, by proclamation, notified us all to that effect. My heart was beating with eager expectation, and I have no doubt the same feeling prevailed with every one present.

"At last Mr. Lorello gave the signal. A few moments of breathless suspense, and then a light flashed up before us, which rendered all around us and as far as the eye could reach, as bright as day. Then a shout arose, a long-drawn continuous shout of exultant joy. We saw before us a broad, straight belt of brilliant light, as brilliant as the sun itself, stretching to the left, far, far away, until it finally dissolved into indistinct clouds of light, when it yet was reflected on the sky. To the right it also stretched far away, but not endless. We could yet see sharp and clear the angle and two lines of the square. Beyond that and far, far off, right before us, it likewise melted into clouds of light, and the reflection hovered like an aurora above it in the sky.

"We heard some cries of pain. Quite a number of persons, in their excitement, forgetting the admonition of Mr. Lorello, had pushed back the blue spectacles, and the glaring light struck their eyes like a destructive acid. They held their eyes with both hands; they had to be carried back and attended to by physicians. Although they suffer great pain, yet it is to be hoped that their eyesight may be saved.

Looking Beyond. 97

"Then we mounted the electric lightning car, and about an hour's ride brought us so far out, that we could see in furthest distance to the left the other angle and two sides of the other square. The reflection of the light still further off indicated that the geometrical figure was complete. Thus the grand object was accomplished, a perfect success.

"We rode back to headquarters and the various workers to their respective camps, where the rest of the night will be spent in general rejoicing. Just returned to headquarters, I send off this telegram. My colleagues of the International Council will do the same to their respective countries. To-morrow we will return to Constantinople."

Mr. Lorello's telegram was shorter. In matter-of-fact language he reported the successful accomplishment of his task. He likewise stated, that after this only a limited number of men of each country would be required to keep the electric works going, to patrol the geometrical figure on electric cars during daytime and make the necessary repairs. They will all move together into two camps. The bulk of the various armies would commence in a day or two to embark for home. The sick, most of whom are convalescent, will be benefited by the sea voyage. Half of those remaining should be relieved in three months by new comers, to be continued thus, in order that always half of the garrison were accustomed to the task and the climate. He sent the same report to all confederate nations.

And so at last the day arrived when our army returned from their glorious campaign.

What are all the campaigns of Cyrus and Alexander, Cæsar, Alaric, Charlemagne, the campaigns of the crusaders, of the first Napoleon, of Grant and Moltke—what are they compared with this brilliant campaign of labour in the cause of science!

That day was a general holiday.

Our gardens were literally devastated. Not a flower was left in any one; but the streets and houses, and more so our club palaces and the grand opera house, were decked with them. An immense triumphal arch of great architectural beauty was erected at the landing.

They had been signalised, and an expecting multitude watched their coming.

Where is the poet laureate whose panegyric would be so powerful as justly to describe that shouting of welcome, that waving of handkerchiefs, while the ship flew swiftly into the harbour, renewed again and again as if it never would end, when they landed!

That marching up to the opera house to the lively strains of music, amidst the acclamations of their rejoicing fellow-citizens and almost smothered with flowers!

The bronzed faces of our campaigners, even of the ladies, gave evidence of what they had undergone. The sick had mostly so far recovered that they could march in the procession, although some of them had to lean on their stronger comrades, and but a few had to carried in litters.

The front seats in the grand opera house had been reserved for the returned volunteers. The curtain was up, and the stage was beautifully decorated. Broad steps led up to the stage on the two ends, and the principal officers and all the judges were assembled there.

The whole orchestra of two hundred musicians gave a fine performance of the popular song, "WELCOME!" with its sweet adagios and rousing *fortissime*. After the last sounds had died away, the Chief Justice stepped to the front. He spoke a short but feeling address to the returned campaigners, and then read the proclamation of the president, rendering the thanks of the nation to the brave volunteers in the cause of science. He next requested them to come up on the stage, ten at a time, to receive the badge of honour.

The orchestra struck up the rousing march, "THE INTERNATIONAL BADGE OF HONOUR," composed for the occasion by Frank Ricardeau, in New Orleans; and the volunteers, ten at a time, walked up the stairs to the immense bower of many-coloured flowers, where they received each the badge and a very elaborately executed copy of the NATION'S THANKS. The greatest order prevailed. As fast as they were decorated, they marched down the other stairs and took their seats again.

When this was over, the officers and judges retired to the rear, and a number of ladies and gentlemen entered, the professional singers of the Grand Opera. An elderly gentleman with grey whiskers preceded them. With a few motions of his hand he assigned them their places, and then he stepped down to the orchestra, where the leader resigned his place to him. Edith whispered to me that this gentleman was Mr. Charles Mayer, the celebrated composer, who on this occasion personally directed the performance of his latest work, the grand oratorio, "Science and Labour Rule the Earth."

What a wonderful composition, and what an exact and beautiful performance! I was so enraptured that Edith had to arouse me when the performance was over. This closed the official part; but the festivities were kept up in the various club-houses all over the city.

We paid a visit to the Machinist Club House on special invitation of Mr. Fest. It was a pleasure to see him and his young wife together. How devoted they were to each other, and with what expressions of tender love his eyes beamed on her! He was entirely cured of his love to her sister. He shook hands with the latter and chatted pleasantly, without showing any emotion whatever.

When I entered the lecture room on the following day, I could not help saying to Mr. Forest: "What do you say now? It does not look as if the people were mentally degenerating for the want of intellectual exercise."

Mr. Forest merely shrugged his shoulders and said: "Facts prove nothing." The poor man is incurable.

I cultivated a warm friendship with Mr. Bowen, the professor of astronomy. Every Sunday I spent a few hours with him on the observatory; Edith and her parents were generally with me. He often turned the telescope on Mars, and we never got tired admiring that triangle. One Sunday we were visiting him again. As usual, he turned the telescope on Mars and took a peep through it; but this time he jumped up and uttered an exclamation. Then he looked again. Long, long time he gazed into it; suddenly he left it and said: "There's the answer." He wrote a few lines in furious haste, then rushed into the telegraph room and called on his assistant to send off the telegram to Washington immediately.

I looked into the telescope, and an exclamation of surprise likewise escaped my lips. Sure enough, there was the answer. The triangle was there yet, *but clear and bright shone the square of the hypotenuse.* We and the inhabitants of Mars have constructed the PYTHAGOREAN PROPOSITION together. We have shown them the squares of the two sides, and they have shown to us the square of the hypotenuse, which is equal to the sum of the squares of the sides.

The wonderful discovery soon was known all over

Boston, and the rush to see it was so great, that the people had to stand in ranks five abreast, the last of them at one time being six blocks off.

The newspapers on the following morning showed us that again Boston had the honour of being first in discovering, and this time Professor Bowen could conscientiously claim it personally. Numerous were the suggestions and propositions made about our next venture. At present it seems that Professor Bowen's proposal has the most advocates.

He says, the fact that Mars is inhabited by thinking beings wishing to correspond with us being established, there would be no necessity for such haste at such sacrifice in signalling to them again. Smaller dimensions could be adopted, too; for we may be sure that for years to come the Mars inhabitants would watch with closest inspection that particular spot on our earth, as we assuredly watch theirs; so that with plenty time before us, thrice the present garrison at the Nile might be sufficient for the future development. The most important thing for the Mars people to know, he says, would be what kind of beings we Earth people are. Therefore he would propose to have the outlines of two persons, a man and a woman, represented by electric lights in the style of pen-pictures, having a length of one hundred and ninety miles, respectively. The posts bearing the lamps which should represent the outlines of these figures should at first be so arranged as to show them in their nude form. The posts bearing the lamps meant to show the outlines of their dress should be added afterward; and the three kinds—the posts showing the line common to dressed and undressed figures—the posts marking the difference of the dressed, and those marking the difference of the undressed ones—these three kinds should have their wire connection with the electric works separately. Thus it could be arranged that at first the two figures would represent man and woman in their nude state, and at any given time, by withholding the current from one set and connecting it with the other, they could be changed into man and woman wearing the dress of the day.

There is all probability that Mr. Bowen's plan will be carried out, and, if continued, in the course of centuries, there may be an established constant communication with the inhabitants of Mars.

Thus I take leave of my readers for the present.

APPENDIX.

The foregoing was in print already, when Edith's friend, Mary Brown, came up quite breathlessly, telling her in joyful excitement that her husband's invention is completed, and an entire success, and that next Wednesday week he will experiment with it before the public at the Grand Opera House.

What a glorious time we are living in!

THE END.

Utopian Literature

AN ARNO PRESS/NEW YORK TIMES COLLECTION

Adams, Frederick Upham.
President John Smith; The Story of a Peaceful Revolution. 1897.

Bird, Arthur.
Looking Forward: A Dream of the United States of the Americas in 1999. 1899.

[Blanchard, Calvin.]
The Art of Real Pleasure. 1864.

Brinsmade, Herman Hine.
Utopia Achieved: A Novel of the Future. 1912.

Caryl, Charles W.
New Era. 1897.

Chavannes, Albert.
The Future Commonwealth. 1892.

Child, William Stanley.
The Legal Revolution of 1902. 1898.

Collens, T. Wharton.
Eden of Labor; or, The Christian Utopia. 1876.

Cowan, James.
Daybreak. A Romance of an Old World. 1896. 2nd ed.

Craig, Alexander.
Ionia; Land of Wise Men and Fair Women. 1898.

Daniel, Charles S.
AI: A Social Vision. 1892.

Devinne, Paul.
The Day of Prosperity: A Vision of the Century to Come. 1902.

Edson, Milan C.
Solaris Farm. 1900.

Fuller, Alvarado M.
A. D. 2000. 1890.

Geissler, Ludwig A.
Looking Beyond. 1891.

Hale, Edward Everett.
How They Lived in Hampton. 1888.

Hale, Edward Everett.
Sybaris and Other Homes. 1869.

Harris, W. S.
Life in a Thousand Worlds. 1905.

Henry, W. O.
Equitania. 1914.

Hicks, Granville, with Richard M. Bennett.
The First to Awaken. 1940.

Lewis, Arthur O., editor
American Utopias: Selected Short Fiction. 1790–1954.

McGrady, Thomas.
Beyond the Black Ocean. 1901.

Mendes H. Pereira.
Looking Ahead. 1899.

Michaelis, Richard.
Looking Further Forward. An Answer to *Looking Backward* by Edward Bellamy. 1890.

Moore, David A.
The Age of Progress. 1856.

Noto, Cosimo.
The Ideal City. 1903.

Olerich, Henry.
A Cityless and Countryless World. 1893.

Parry, David M.
The Scarlet Empire. 1906.

Peck, Bradford.
The World a Department Store. 1900.

Reitmeister, Louis Aaron.
If Tomorrow Comes. 1934.

Roberts, J. W.
Looking Within. 1893.

Rosewater, Frank.
'96; A Romance of Utopia. 1894.

Satterlee, W. W.
Looking Backward and What I Saw. 2nd ed. 1890.

Schindler, Solomon.
Young West; A Sequel to Edward Bellamy's Celebrated Novel "Looking Backward." 1894.

Smith, Titus K.
Altruria. 1895.

Steere, C. A.
When Things Were Doing. 1908.

Taylor, William Alexander.
Intermere. 1901.

Thiusen, Ismar.
The Diothas, or, A Far Look Ahead. 1883.

Vinton, Arthur Dudley.
Looking Further Backward. 1890.

Wooldridge, C. W.
Perfecting the Earth. 1902.

Wright, Austin Tappan.
Islandia. 1942.